THE GRAND FINALE OF BRITISH STEAM

Alan Castle

THE GRAND FINALE OF BRITISH STEAM

First published in the UK in 2013

© Demand Media Limited 2013

www.demand-media.co.uk

Printed and bound in China

ISBN 978-1-909217-63-8

Contents

Introduction

A chronology of 1968

The year of 1968 was a pivotal year in a period of great change and, with the march of so-called 'progress' that included man being a matter of months away from walking on the moon, the time was up for steam. The first week of August was to see the closure of the final three depots - effectively drawing to a conclusion the century and a half of loyal service provided by a form of transport to which the wealth of our nation owed so much. The steam era ended so poignantly on 4 August, a day on which innumerable steam railwaymen, most of whom had dedicated their entire lives to the railways, were declared redundant. These words, therefore, are a tribute to those final men and machines.

On 11 August, did any of those thousands sat in the massive traffic gridlocks up in the high Pennines really believe that this would not be for ever? The, then seemingly unshakeable, view from the exalted heights of BR management was that it was not to return under any circumstances. Indeed, certain individuals then resident on the British Railways Board were so adamantly opposed to steam as to be desirous to see it despatched as soon as was possible... and no matter what the cost!

Indecent haste

Even die-hards accepted that steam had to go one day - but not so hurriedly and with such a disgraceful lack of gratitude, and the indecent haste with

which most of the fleet soon came to be disposed of, was a sad reflection upon the state of our emerging society. Even the few privately preserved locomotives in working order did not represent the image that top management wished to create. The view was that steam was the creation of a more primitive age and, quite simply, deserved no place in an era of new technology. For those who did take the time to cogitate upon such matters, there was a sadness felt that reflected an acceptance that the life as we knew it was soon to change, perhaps for the better, perhaps not, but certainly a realisation that changes were inevitable and counted as 'progress'.

There had been a period in the immediate post-war years, during which attempts were made to construct modern and more reliable steam locomotives as the way forward for the then newly nationalised railway, rather than to leap headlong into untried and untested dieselisation. In the pages to follow, we shall discover why this was and how things then suddenly changed, both as a consequence of the 1955 Modernisation Plan, and also because of the effects of the later decimation of the national network, as initiated by the infamous Dr Beeching. Despite the ambitious aspirations of the British Transport Commission design teams, many new locomotives ultimately came to be sent for scrap well before their 10th birthdays. Some were hardly 'run-in' – clearly, a shocking and disgraceful waste!

Until as late as 1967, the steam-age railway in the North West of England, in many respects, really did still remain relatively untouched. North of Preston, steam working still continued - and in some quantity – particularly on the remoter moorland main line stretches over Shap and along the Settle & Carlisle line, where, in both places, even large Pacifics were still very much in evidence. However, when Carlisle Kingmoor, Tebay and Workington depots finally closed to steam working on 31 December, this proved to be a dramatic and major downturn in steam's sphere of operation. Maurice Burns made a sentimental journey to witness first-hand the very last steam workings over Shap Summit. After 122 years, it really was the end of an era and Maurice provides some fitting words in appreciation. His own personal epitaph encompasses, in particular, the passing of one essential, but otherwise little-addressed, aspect of railway operation – the men and locomotives of the Shap Bankers.

Come the dawn of the 1968 New Year, the 360-odd steam locomotives nominally still in service at the 'lucky thirteen' surviving depots found themselves basically restricted to essentially short sojourns in and around Lancashire, north Cheshire, a corner of the Peak District and an occasional foray a few miles into West Yorkshire. With no alternative motive power to call upon, staff at depots invariably had to 'make-do-and-mend', often against almost impossible odds with little or no spare parts back-up, just to keep a bare minimum of engines available for traffic. Everywhere that one looked standards of cleanliness had deteriorated noticeably. This, of course, had gradually been taking place for many years and, for some enthusiasts, it became a sad fact of life that having to go to the extreme extent of having to clean one's own engines, if only in order to stand any chance of securing a reasonable photograph, was to become very much a part of the accepted routine. Maurice Burns recounts one or

two of the numerous cleaning sessions in which he personally became involved and Paul Riley continues on a similar theme with a few further words on the last days of the 'Great Steam Chase'... or the trials and tribulations of steam photography in the 1960s.

The noose tightens

For that handful of surviving depots still in business, the noose was ever-tightening. The first three to go, all on 4 March, were Trafford Park, Buxton and Northwich, the latter two being at the extremities of the route traversed by intensive limestone minerals traffic. These closing weeks fortunately coincided with some very wintry conditions in the Peak District which, when trains actually were able to run, did provide some spectacular photo opportunities. Within another couple of months, four further depots succumbed, with Stockport Edgeley, Heaton Mersey, Edge Hill and Speke Junction closing on 6 May 1968. It was a near miracle that steam survived to such an advanced stage as May regularly hauling a prestigious titled train. Nevertheless, despite more than one previous attempt at dieselisation, Stanier 'Black Fives' remained firmly on the roster of the 'Belfast Boat Express'. We examine the reasons behind this and hear about some of the more outstanding runs.

Elsewhere, life went on much as it always had done and nowhere more so than in the Yorkshire Dales. The limestone traffic from quarries on the former Skipton-Grassington Branch took ballast trains to destinations from which steam had otherwise long-vanished and we follow one such train on an outing to Appleby. The remaining three depots in the Manchester Division; Newton Heath, Patricroft and Bolton closed at the very end of June and Steve Leyland provides an account of the demise of his own local shed of Bolton.

The final three

With but a single month to go, this chronology is brought to a conclusion with an in-depth focus upon 'The Final Three'. During those final hectic weeks, the otherwise totally unassuming and quite 'matter of fact' steam depots at Carnforth, Lostock Hall and Rose Grove had fame literally thrust upon them and the area around soon became inundated with visitors of totally unprecedented proportions. Right up until the very last weekend of all, it was still possible to travel on one or other of two 'portions' of main-line expresses that, from Preston, completed their final few miles onwards to their destinations behind steam power. Tom Heavyside provides a personal insight to the final passenger workings of 3 August.

Most of the special train activity in the closing weeks concentrated upon the last day, when each of the major railtour operators of the time vied for custom with their individual 'Farewell to Steam' sorties. With severely limited itineraries being available and with the, perhaps inevitable, Sunday late-running scenarios, on 4 August it soon became almost impossible for those witnessing events to predict from which direction the next special would appear! Published here, for the first time ever, is a comprehensive list of all the footplate crews involved in that historic day.

One week later, three 5MTs and a Britannia were engaged in operating various stages of a BR-organised final steam excursion upon which history has since imparted the infamous sobriquet, 'The Fifteen Guinea Special'. Some reflections upon that historic day are provided from three very differing viewpoints - a passenger, a 'linesider' and a footplate inspector involved in the behind-the-scenes planning and preparations.

After it really was all over and the masses had departed, what happened then? As we now know, a handful of engines - from all three depots - survived the cutting torch, but there was no escape for the remainder. A few lingered on for some months, rusting away in forlorn lines awaiting their inevitable destiny, but the 'Barry phenomenon' was really some years to the future and with neither the funding being available, nor the preservation mania yet really having taken off, all would eventually be towed away for scrap. With the end of steam, so also disappeared most of the steam age infrastructure and, as a postscript to those unforgettable final months, Robert Gregson visited the derelict and decaying remains of Lostock Hall shed which, remarkably, survived for 22 years after its last steam locomotive had departed.

No 44993 Copy Pit

Chapter 1

British Railways 1948-1968...
The first 20 years

It must have occurred sometime around the springtime of 1956 when, from a primary school playground on the outskirts of Preston, I glimpsed my very first main line diesel locomotive. Although very few youngsters growing up in such halcyon days of steam could really pretend to appreciate much of what was happening, that vision witnessed from the little schoolyard in Middleforth really was a portent of the future railway as this was to evolve.

At that period in time, of course, British Railways possessed just seven examples

and the pioneer LMS Co-Co, No 10000, had actually been constructed some time previously, in 1948. Having sojourned for much of their earlier years on the Southern Region, No 10000 and its twin No 10001 had now returned to their earlier stamping grounds. Not long afterwards, they came to be joined by another three former SR stable-mates, in the form of the Bulleid-designed Co-Cos Nos 10201/2/3, all of which soon came to truly exemplify the astonishingly swift metamorphosis from steam to diesel that was so very imminent.

The age of the steam railway. The decision to develop existing steam power had been made as long ago as 1948, being greatly influenced at that time by the parlous state of Britain's economy and the low capital-cost necessary in preference to massive expenditure required to get large-scale and totally untested dieselisation off the ground. One of the 999 'Standards' that came to be constructed by British Railways between 1951 and 1960, Class 4MT 4-6-0 No 75019 passes through Rose Grove station in April 1968, en-route to Skipton to take up its duties on 'No 94 Target' – which will involve working a train of new ballast from the quarries at Spencers Sidings on the Grassington branch.

British Railways' standardisation of steam

On 1 January 1948, Britain's railways had been nationalised and the newly created 'British Railways' had come to inherit more than 20,000 steam locomotives from the 'Big Four' companies (as well as some other smaller railways that went into public ownership at the same time). Over the course of the next 12 years, production of steam continued apace with, initially, many pre-nationalisation classes being perpetuated, until designs for new BR Standard classes were unveiled in 1951. These were largely based on LMS practice, but incorporating ideas and modifications from other constituent companies and, in some respects, also from North America - characteristic features being taper boilers, high running plates, two cylinders, rocker grates and streamlined cabs.

A total of 999 'Standards' came to be constructed between 1951 and 1960. In addition, more than 750 ex-WD locomotives were also taken into stock; many having seen service abroad during World War II. Remarkably, within just 20 short years, even all of these much newer engines had gone and steam was dead.

This part of the story really begins on 25 January 1955 with the announcement of a £1240-million Modernisation Plan, spelling-out the British Transport Commission's scheme for large-scale modernisation of the rail network, the principle feature of which was to be the ultimate total replacement of steam by diesel and electric traction. Naturally, diesels were still something of a novelty, but, nevertheless, following soon after the Plan was published, the proposed 1956 Building Programme for steam came to be drastically slashed. From a total of 263 proposed engines deleted from the previous schedule, these included 36 additional Britannia Pacifics - for three Regions, 20 Clan Pacifics for the North Eastern Region and the first of a new Class 8F

2-8-0 design. Notwithstanding the transparently clear 'writing-on-the-wall' for steam, a further few did actually come to be constructed - these comprising 84 9F 2-10-0s and 61 mixed traffic engines of various types – all authorised as an 'additional build'.

In the event, it was to be the former GWR Swindon Works that assumed the honour of turning out the very last of that final order. Taking longer than expected to complete its batch of 9F 2-10-0s, No 92220 Evening Star only came to be released to traffic in as late as March 1960. With its copper-capped double chimney and other Swindon embellishments (such as being the only named 9F), it naturally found itself allocated to the Western Region. With careful maintenance, the majority of these brand-new and modern machines could probably have worked for up to 50 years. Nevertheless, the first withdrawals were not far away and, ultimately, it was all proven to have been a quite shocking waste.

The question did beg asking as to why such large numbers had actually been constructed, particularly when it was already known that their usefulness would be limited to such a few short years. But, the BTC's decision to develop existing steam power had been made as long ago as 1948, being greatly influenced at the time by the parlous state of Britain's economy and the low capital-cost necessary to build a series of new steam, in preference to the massive expenditure required to get large-scale and, of course, totally untested, dieselisation off the ground. Within eight years and following the radical changes ensuing, no sooner had the first batch of 32 Class 9Fs been completed at Crewe in December 1954, than the bottom-line of the Modernisation Plan dictated the total obliteration of steam. Although the BTC had previously pushed ahead in good faith, the argument for coal and steam, based on cheap fuel and efficiency, was very soon to be lost. Coal was becoming more and more expensive and the otherwise ageing fleet of steam power was becoming increasingly difficult to maintain.

Figures produced claimed to show that the cost of crewing and fuelling a steam locomotive was some 2½ times that of diesel power, and the daily mileage achievable was far lower, as well. As labour costs rose, particularly after World War II, non-steam technologies had become much more cost-efficient.

This was a trend by no means restricted to the UK for, by the end of the 1970s, most Western countries had completely replaced steam in passenger service and very soon afterwards likewise those remaining in freight usage.

Progress and the decline of steam

Before any final decision was taken regarding bulk delivery of the anticipated 2500 diesel locomotives required, British Railways had stated that they wished to spend time evaluating the results of the diesel experiment. A 'pilot scheme' of about 170 examples was to be constructed for design assessment. Orders were placed with many different locomotive builders (the majority of whom possessed absolutely no experience of main-line locomotive construction) and prototypes came to be hastily 'cobbled together' essentially for this evaluation. However, the project then came to be abandoned under pressure from the Conservative government, resulting in BR having no real option but to place large orders for unproven machines and with designs straight off the drawing board. Sadly, many steam engines which were less than ten years old came to be sacrificed in the ensuing totally unnecessary haste, but some of the diesel classes that replaced steam soon proved to be so unreliable that they saw even less service than their immediate forebears. Some transformation that proved to be!

Furthermore, the infamous Dr Beeching had also chopped the national rail network down in size by a third. The scale of changes occurring can be gauged from the fact that, the 20,000 or more steam engines in service up until the late 1950s, came to be replaced by a mere 5000 diesels and electrics.

That ceaseless march towards total dieselisation/electrification gradually ensued and the soon-to-be-termed 'British Rail' coined such titles as 'Inter-City' and gradually painted all of its carriages blue and grey, this presumably in an early attempt to present a 'corporate image' that was thought vital to accompany its new trains. Naturally, steam engines had no place in such visions, for they were too obviously mechanical, labour-intensive and possessed embarrassing and allegedly unhealthy emissions.

The demise of steam came at different times around the country. East Anglia had become largely dieselised by the end of the 1950s, with all bar one remaining steam depot having closed by 1962. With some notable exceptions, much of Scotland north of Glasgow and Edinburgh also saw steam give way to diesel traction by 1962, while Western Region steam faded into the history books at the end of 1965 with the Southern and North Eastern Regions following suit in 1967.

The release back to traffic from Crewe Works, on 2 February 1967, of Britannia Pacific No 70013 Oliver Cromwell proved to be the very last steam locomotive to receive an overhaul at any BR workshop. From that date forward, the by now vastly reduced number of surviving railway workshops were to concentrate merely on the maintenance of diesel/electric traction. Any overhauls necessary to keep steam engines in traffic had to be undertaken at those few depots still with equipment and machinery capable of doing such work. Clearly, boiler-lifts and heavy overhauls were out of the question, even by those prepared to retain their alliance with steam.

No more spare components were to be manufactured, or even refurbished, and if a part could not be cannibalised from elsewhere, depots were faced with no other option but to withdraw locomotives for scrapping.

The first day of January 1968 was to dawn with but about 360 steam locomotives remaining in service at a mere 13 depots – all situated in the North West of England and this is where we take up the story.

All that epitomised the archetypal country station goods yard, that had existed almost unaltered since the 19th Century, can be seen somewhere in this superb picture. Rose Grove shed's Stanier 8F 2-8-0 No 48423 has paused between shunting duties at Kirkham, while in the course of working 'No 25 Target' which trips between Blackpool North and Preston NU Yard. Seen storming away from the station is Lostock Hall's 'Black Five' No 45444 at the head of the 12:44 Preston to Blackpool South – a through portion of the 09:05 from London Euston. The road coach is one of the Ribble Motor Company's 'Burlingham Seagull' bodied Leyland Tiger Cubs built in 1956 and is, presumably, providing transport for a permanent way gang employed in the neighbourhood. Some Sunday work in the area is clearly anticipated, as the sidings contain wagons of fresh ballast that have undoubtedly originated from quarries on the Grassington Branch.

Chapter 2

Last of the Shap bankers

Steam over Shap ended on 31 December 1967

The railways across the northern fells have always held a special fascination for me and none more so than that over Shap Fell with steam. In the early 1960s, railway periodicals were liberally sprinkled with photographic masterpieces recorded by those such as the late Eric Treacy and Derek Cross. A superb landscape and memorable visions of steam engines working hard were, after all, the perfect combination, especially if the weather was kind! Indeed, the sight and sound of a heavy northbound train, with locomotives both on the front and also at the rear, toiling up the Shap incline, was one of the finest displays of raw steam power one could see – a truly unforgettable experience. It was against this background that I, and countless other enthusiasts, headed for these parts at

After a night-time snowfall, a weak wintry sun is barely over the towering mass of Langdale Fell as 'Black Five' No 44884 with safety valves blowing-off slowly moves forward onto the hill with a Christmas extra parcels working. Providing some much-needed muscle at the rear is Fairburn 2-6-4T No 42210. In the distance, another 2-6-4T prepares to leave the shed to bank a following train.

the end of BR steam to capture on film those images of steam that would soon be no more.

My own Shap memories spanned just three years, starting on a hot summer's day in August 1964, but did leave a lasting impression. I had reached the summit cutting the hard way from my home on Teesside, on my 'Jack Taylor' cycle, arriving just after lunch. For the next four hours, there followed a procession of steam; these including a 4F light-engine, a Duchess No 46245 City of London, a filthy Britannia No 70013 Oliver Cromwell, a 9F on a Ford car train, a Jubilee and a large handful of Class 5s on freights. I had hoped to see some trains banked up the incline but, remarkably, on this, my first visit here, none of these required a banker. Just my luck!

LEFT A Fairburn 4MT 2-6-4 tank comes off Tebay shed, to buffer-up against the rear of a Stanier 'Black Five' -hauled freight patiently waiting under the shadow of Loups Fell ready to do battle with the four miles of 1-in-75 to the summit

LAST OF THE SHAP BANKERS

BELOW During the bitterly cold night of 27 November 1964, the two engines on Shap banking duties, Fairburn 4MT 2-6-4 tanks Nos 42110 and 42210, take a short break in the yard in between turns up the hill

However, all that was to change on my next visit to Tebay (another cycle ride), this time on a Friday evening after work, on 27 November 1964. For the crossing of Stainmore, the weather had been perfect and I arrived at Tebay just before midnight. My first visit to the shed would not be forgotten in a hurry, it created such a huge impact, with the noise of exhausts and whistling in the darkness throughout the night. There was just so much traffic at that time, either speeding south downhill or heavy freights stopping for a banker and then restarting.

There were two banking-engines on duty, Fairburn 2-6-4 tanks Nos 42210 and 42110, which were both sat outside the 'bothy' ready for action. Inside the bothy, the enginemen made me most welcome; they were such a friendly bunch and, as I sat round the coal fire drinking tea, I heard a freight slowly plod through the station, then on to the foot of the bank to whistle up for a banker. The driver and fireman went outside and, climbing aboard No 42210, moved off the shed and eased up to the guards van at the rear of the freight. Following the customary exchange of whistles, the train disappeared noisily up the bank and into the darkness. Just how the people in Tebay ever slept, I will never know!

Moments later, another

freight, hauled by one of the last of the Patriots, No 45531 Sir Frederick Harrison, whistled for assistance and it was now that the driver of banker No 42110 offered me a trip to the summit. After the buffers of the tank engine touched the guards van and following the exchanging of whistles, it was soon full-regulator for the banker.

Looking forward into the darkness, there was so much exhaust noise and almost constant shovelling of coal into the firebox by the poor fireman, that the Patriot at the front could not be heard at all.

Indeed, we joked that the crew were taking it easy and leaving all the work for the banker! After the Scout Green 'box, we were soon passing the distant lights of Shap Wells Hotel and into the steep-sided summit cutting. Approaching the then Summit signalbox, the driver of No 42110 slammed shut the regulator and, slowly, the guards van tail-light moved away and, as if by magic, we could now hear in the distance the exhaust of the Patriot at the front end of the freight. A quick descent of the bank followed, to discover another freight with a Class 5 waiting for assistance. I did two more trips up to the summit, but as 03:00 approached, tiredness set in and, in the warmth of the locomen's bothy, I crashed-out in my sleeping bag!

ABOVE Well into the climb, Stanier 'Black Five' No 45312, banked at the rear by a Standard Class 4MT, battles against the gradient and a stiff easterly wind as it passes Greenholme with a northbound fully fitted freight

LAST OF THE SHAP BANKERS

RIGHT For those who enjoy the great outdoors, there is no wilder place than the southern slopes of Shap Fell. This bleak and forlorn stretch of moorland is one of howling winds and horizontal rainfalls, where only ragged sheep and railway photographers might roam. With one of Tebay's Standard Class 4MT 4-6-0s working hard at the rear, for Springs Branch's Stanier 'Black Five' No 45321 the hard work is nearly over as it approaches Shap Wells with a summer Saturday Euston-Glasgow relief

The next morning, I could not believe my eyes - it was snowing! However, by mid-morning, the sky had totally cleared and I cycled up to Shap Wells, where I caught several Class 5s on freights or parcel trains, all banked by the Fairburn tanks.

The lighting conditions were perfect,

with a combination of snow, sun and steam! For black and white pictures, I used a 35mm Practica camera, some being taken with my new 135mm telephoto lens, while, for Kodachrome slides, I was also fortunate to have brought my father's British-made Ilford Advocate camera.

Throughout 1965, I made many more return visits; often it has to be said, in dreadful weather! However, I made a conscious decision several times to travel on the banking engines in daylight to take photographs from the footplate. Getting a footplate ride was easy - one just had to ask! Tebay shed staff were a friendly bunch and nothing was too much trouble. So, once more, I travelled on the footplate of No 42110.

The heavy freight traffic always required a banker, but one train stands in particular. It was immense. I do not know its exact weight, but it could have been about 1000 tons, consisting of a riding van, a crane and a long train of concrete track panels intended for re-laying the West Coast Main Line. Hauled by two 8F 2-8-0s at the front, both with a full head of steam, and with a Fairburn tank at the rear, this train passed me at Greenholme cutting

at just walking pace, about 5mph, but the crews and engines were in full command of the job, reaching the summit without stopping.

By 1967, the type of banking engines had changed. The 1960s had started out with a stud of Fowler 2-6-4 tanks, but these came to be displaced by the Fairburns in 1964. As the latter, in turn, became worn out, they were ultimately replaced by BR Standard Class 4 4-6-0 tender engines.

These were to become the last steam banking engines at Tebay; this prior to the end of steam at Carlisle and the closure of Kingmoor and Tebay sheds from 1 January 1968. While man enough for the job, compared to the Fowler and Fairburn tanks, they proved not to be so popular with the Tebay crews, due to the draughty cabs when tender-first descending from Shap! First to arrive, in April 1967, were Nos 75019, 75026 (fitted with double chimney), 75027 and 75039.

A month later, Nos 75024, 75030, 75032 and 75035 were added to the allocation. Nos 75035 and 75039 did not last long and were soon withdrawn, but the remainder lasted to the very end of steam at the shed.

After closure of Tebay, Nos 75019 and 75027 saw further service at Carnforth, indeed right until the very end of steam on BR in August 1968. Happily, one Tebay banking engine is still with us today, in the form of No 75027 - now preserved on the Bluebell Railway.

Towards the end of 1967, in the last months of steam over Shap, the chances of getting any more decent photographs of the bankers were rare. Carlisle Kingmoor shed (12A) had a declining number of working locomotives and, with closure occurring during the Christmas holiday period, it was hard to pin down the very last workings. However, all of a sudden, along the grapevine travelled news of a football excursion from Carlisle to Blackpool and back… planned to run on Boxing Day.

Looking back upon how this actually happened, it being before the days of the internet, emails and mobile phones, is quite amazing! We even knew the booked motive power. It was scheduled to be the last working Britannia,

No 70013 Oliver Cromwell – the special leaving Carlisle about 10:00 and returning after dark at about 21:00.

During the evening of Christmas Day and that night, ten or so photographers descended on Kingmoor shed to seek out No 70013 and to give it a thorough cleaning with oil and paraffin. It would be one of the engine's last Kingmoor working, prior to movement to Carnforth to work out its last days before the end of steam on BR on 11 August 1968.

Boxing Day morning was a photographer's dream. Full sun, a clear blue sky… and a frost! Now with a super-shine finish, Oliver Cromwell looked superb – could this really be the last BR steam working ever over Shap from Carlisle?

Most opted for the curves at Strickland Woods, south of Penrith. The accompanying pictures explain it all. With the pictures 'in the bag' and with no other steam trains to photograph, everyone went home happy. We had seen what was likely to be the last steam over Shap… and in perfect conditions.

That should have been the end of this story but, for me, it was not quite. While sat back at home on Teesside having my tea, I thought, Oliver Cromwell will be on the return working in just four hours' time and, really, I should be there, if only to make a tape-recording

of the train climbing towards the summit for the very last time. Should I go all the way back to Shap - that was the question? It would be far easier to take the easy option and to remain at home? Well, I did make the effort and I have never regretted it – coming to witness what turned out to be a memorable spectacle.

In darkness, I arrived at lonely Scout Green signalbox. There was little traffic on the evening of Boxing Day and the friendly signalman appreciated the company, offering to let me know when the return football excursion was due. Eventually, I got the word that No 70013 was passing Grayrigg 'box, so, with my Phillips reel-to-reel tape-recorder and torch, I then walked up the line beyond the 'box.

It was a magical evening... especially for such an occasion as this. While it was dark, there was no wind, a clear sky, stars above and a heavy frost. Indeed, it was so quiet, you could hear a pin drop! I listened for the sound of a train in the distance, expecting to hear the distant roar of Oliver Cromwell in the Lune Gorge below, as it gathered speed to charge the bank of Shap. What I heard, though, was just a faint rumble and then... total silence. This could only mean one thing... Oliver Cromwell had stopped for a banker!

There would appear to be just one snag. On Tebay shed, all the fires appeared to have been dropped, so there was no banker available.

No 70013 would now have to tackle Shap with its heavy train, from a standing start.

I heard the chime whistle faintly in the distance, then the first beat of the exhaust but, soon, the engine was accelerating up to 30mph by Greenholme - the noise being so loud in the still night air, the regulator was obviously 'in the roof'.

After Greenholme cutting, the train came into view, with the glow of the firebox reflecting in the exhaust and the illuminated carriage lights in the distance.

It was certainly going well, as it approached Scout Green 'box, with occasional sparks going skyward from the chimney. Just as it had passed me, it went into a slight wheelspin, which was quickly brought under control by the driver, before eventually regaining its feet and plodding over the summit at over 20mph.

I had, therefore, witnessed every beat of Oliver Cromwell from a standing start in Tebay Station to Shap Summit - a memory I will never forget! As the train passed over the summit and accelerated on towards Penrith, it eventually went totally silent again... steam over Shap and the banking engines were now no more.

31 December 1967 marked not only the end of steam over the Northern Fells, but also, sadly, the real end of main line steam in Britain.

The last remaining steam engines on BR were now to be concentrated in a small area in the North West, with no real place to go, but, for many enthusiasts such as myself, the great memories of BR steam over Shap - with its banking engines - live on.

Boxing Day 1967 and the last southbound steam passenger working over Shap rounds the curve through Strickland woods headed by No 70013 Oliver Cromwell. In the darkness of a frosty winter's evening, Maurice would be a lone spectator later this day at the lonely Scout Green signalbox to witness the return working of this Carlisle-Blackpool football special climbing the bank unassisted.

Chapter 3

'To a dignified end'

The last engine cleaners on British Railways

In the final years of BR steam, thousands of enthusiasts travelled from one part of the UK to another, as each region saw its last engines disappear for scrap. Most would carry a camera and take the odd shed or station photograph. However, with engines in quite appalling condition mechanically, many had been patched up using parts from other withdrawn locomotives and, although each shed had 'cleaners', these had stopped cleaning engines long before the end of steam. For freight engines in particular, the only time that these were seen to be clean was when they had been repainted following works' overhauls, but that was now a long time ago…

There were one or two exceptions, where shedmasters took a pride in keeping their locomotives clean and where cleaners did do the job for which they had been employed. The differing management styles were never more obvious and starkly apparent than during the well-documented 'Indian Summer' of the A4 Pacifics, running between Glasgow and Aberdeen. Here, one could see freshly cleaned Aberdeen Ferryhill A4s passing filthy ones from Glasgow St Rollox which had not seen cleaning rags for many a year.

Aberdeen did clean its A4s right to the very end and, when its last LNER pacific, No 60532 Blue Peter, was retained on standby duties until December 1966, this, too, remained clean until withdrawal.

It was against this background that,

The cleaning of one's first steam engine is something one would never forget - especially when this was an A4! Being caught in the process by the Perth MPD running foreman in August 1965, equally memorable was the fact that he did not throw us off the shed, but did want his picture taken! Here he proudly poses in front of A4 No 60027 Merlin while Dave Hartas (left) and Paul Riley continue with their task unabated!

in July 1965, while on a holiday near Perth, I bumped into the late Paul Riley - a great guy who shared my passion of going to that little bit extra in order to capture on film the last of BR steam. We were both fans of the late WJV (Bill)

Anderson and his style of photography and how we envied the chance to photograph immaculate Pacifics at exotic locations, such as Glenfarg Bank in Fife, much as Bill had so often done.

Just then, a truly filthy A4 – No 60027

BELOW The transformation of the filthiest A4 ever seen is now complete and the crew prepare their engine for an early afternoon Perth to Edinburgh passenger departure over Glenfarg Bank

Merlin passed by. Once the immaculate pride of Haymarket and frequently working 'The Elizabethan', it had now been relegated to work out its final days at St Margaret's, on freight or occasional passenger work. At Perth this day, it had been booked to work the 14:55 to Edinburgh, over Glenfarg, so Paul suggested we clean it up ourselves!

In the chapter 'Never Again', later in this book, Paul describes in detail what actually happened, but, suffice to say, in itself, for me it was a momento

us event to clean an A4. This would however lead, in future years, to meeting up with numerous other enthusiasts, all of whom possessed the same drive and guts to get their hands dirty if necessary, in order to transform filthy engines back to their former glory – and all in the interests of photography!

In the final years of steam, we, the enthusiasts, had to become the real - if unofficial - last engine cleaners on BR!

However, with no training, Paul and I leant a few lessons as a consequence of this initial experience. Firstly, we needed to add more bearing oil to the paraffin that we used in order to produce a better shine. Secondly, to avoid friction with crews, we should always dry-off the handrails and tidy-up when finished. We did see our shining A4 climbing the 1-in-75 of Glenfarg, but noticed to our horror that we had left some cleaning rags jammed between the boiler and handrail, right next to the Merlin nameplates. We did not do that again, either!

Paul and I soon came to be joined by an expanding group of like-minded keen photographers, mainly from the

The transformation of the filthiest A4 ever seen is now complete and the crew prepare their engine for an early afternoon Perth to Edinburgh passenger departure over Glenfarg Bank

5 November 1966 saw the end of one of the most popular locomotive classes built by the LNER - the Gresley V2 2-6-2s. The very last working example, No 60836, was scheduled by the Scottish Region to make one final run from Edinburgh Waverley to Perth and Aberdeen, before being sent for scrap. To ensure that it went out in a blaze of glory, the engine was cleaned overnight at Edinburgh St Margaret's shed.

Midlands, who came to nickname themselves the MNA.

The next engine earmarked for cleaning was Dundee's single-chimney A2, No 60530 Sayajirao, which worked a passenger to Glasgow. Following this, we then travelled to Ayr to clean Hughes Fowler 'Crab' 2-6-0 No 42789. With the greater numbers now involved, cleaning became quicker and, at Ayr, we found we could clean more than just the one locomotive.

The first cleaning adventure of 1967 for me turned out to be the last run of the 'Cambrian Coast Express' from Aberystwyth, with steam over Talerddig Summit to Shrewsbury. On 4 March 1967, Paul had organised the event to perfection, this including the borrowing, from a retired former manager of the Cambrian Railways, of the original 'CCE' headboard. Rostered motive power, by this time, no longer being the immaculate Machynlleth Manors, quite filthy Standard 4MT 4-6-0s were provided by Shrewsbury, a shed by now part of the re-vamped London Midland Region. These usually no longer possessed either front number plates or shedplates and, being LMR engines, also had the wrong type of top lamp-bracket for the Western Region headboard!

No problem! A suitable bracket was 'borrowed' from a withdrawn ex-WR 78xxx 2-6-0 at Shrewsbury shed (photographer Alan Castle spent the major part of an uncomfortable night in the empty tender, removing the rusty bolts securing this!). Meanwhile, Chris Weston had organised in York carriage works the manufacture of an 89C shedplate and Dave Williams had made an assortment of different numerals to glue onto a blank number plate – we did not know in advance which engine would be rostered! Half-a-dozen other photographers descended upon Aberystwyth station to clean the engine - at the platform end - with officialdom totally turning a blind eye!

There, in just over an hour, a 75033 number plate was manufactured, shed-plate and new top lamp-bracket fitted, bufferbeam repainted and, using cleaning material brought from Shrewsbury shed on the inward working of No 75033, the loco was transformed. Finally the 'Cambrian Coast Express' headboard was proudly placed in position and, with the assistance of car-borne colleagues, the last run of this famous train was photographed climbing to Talerddig Summit.

Such an event would be a hard act to follow, but I did then discover, right on my own North Eastern doorstep, an idyllic three-mile long steam-hauled passenger branch line running between Alnmouth and Alnwick. At Alnmouth, there was even a small loco shed - a sub-depot of 52D Tweedmouth. Motive power was provided by Peppercorn LNER-design K1 2-6-0s, which had a

layover at the attractive Alnwick station between duties. It was here, on the platform end, that I asked the crew if I could clean their engine – this being the one-time Fort William No 62011.

A few weeks later, I cleaned another one, No 62021, and on that occasion the crew joined in! Even later, in May 1966, upon returning from a weekend in Scotland, I popped into Alnmouth shed, only to discover to my astonishment that one of the very last V2s, No 60836, had been 'acquired' as a result of a motive power shortage, and that it had been rostered to work the two-coach branch passenger. In one hour, the V2 was cleaned up!

Eventually, this superb steam branch line operation went diesel as from 18 June 1966, but not before I had cleaned No 62011 overnight ready for the last day and then posed the entire Alnmouth shed staff in front of it. In the mid-afternoon of that final day, one of Tyne Dock's 9F 2-10-0s, No 92099, turned up - to see steam go out in a blaze of glory. It was filthy, of course, and I hastily suggested to the mass of enthusiasts present, that a rapid cleaning session was desired. This commenced on Alnmouth shed, but,

LEFT In the summer of 1966, the last handful of V2s at Dundee had a regular summer passenger working to Edinburgh Waverley. Having received an overnight facelift on Dundee shed, No 60919 makes a fine sight as it accelerates off the Tay Bridge at Wormit on an August Saturday such was the shortage of time, that the cleaning had to be finished in Alnwick station!

As news of such unofficial activities spread along the grapevine, the cleaning of engines by enthusiasts was gaining momentum. At the time, York shed had on loan Leeds Holbeck's 'Jubilee' No 45675 Hardy for passing-out firemen, this occurring on a York to Newcastle parcels turn. In the event, No 45675 was not only cleaned (in what is now the NRM), but the smokebox and buffer-beams were also totally repainted.

Over in the North West at Carnforth, another group of photographers had discovered that the unique Stephenson-Link 'Black Five' No 44767 was booked for a mid-day Morecambe to Leeds summer Saturday extra passenger. This particular engine cleaned up really well. The photograph, however, of the train climbing to Clapham, was only achieved after the gang had waded through Clapham Beck, the infant River Lune in bare feet, to reach their chosen location!

RIGHT Remarkably, Montrose depot became one of the final outposts of BR steam in Scotland, lasting until March 1967. A sub-shed of Dundee, elderly ex-North British Class J37 0-6-0s were retained here for working the daily freight to Brechin. In September 1966, No 64620, polished overnight to perfection, stands in the old wooden shed, prior to setting out on its daily trip to Brechin

The North British line from Morpeth to Riccarton Junction on the Waverley Route, had been cut back to Woodburn by the 1950s, but, somehow, a Thursdays-only freight survived until closure of the line. Having cleaned ex-NER *J27* 0-6-0 No 65842 on South Blyth shed, at the conclusion of a memorable day's photography, in perfect weather, a group of unofficial engine cleaners, Maurice Burns (left), Paul Riley, Tim Stephens and Dave Gouldthorp, pose on the bufferbeam at Woodburn on 22 September 1966.

By the summer of 1966, every enthusiast was in Scotland, or so it appeared. Steam did not have long to go, yet it still consisted of a remarkably wide variety of engine types, from B1s and V2s, to A2s and A4s, besides some other attractive North British products. Dundee was my favourite shed and, during that summer, its V2s were regularly rostered for a Dundee to Blackpool passenger. V2 No 60813, the one with the mini smoke deflectors, was the booked engine one day and came to receive the full overnight treatment. Seeing their immaculate engine as they turned up for duty, the crew were quite in disbelief. They did, however, kindly arrange some smoke for us as the train came off the Tay Bridge. No 60919 was cleaned for the same duty on yet another occasion. Clearly, this clandestine practice was now becoming commonplace and

The rugged ex-NER J27 0-6-0s had outlasted many more modern machines, even when steam was in rapid decline. By 1967, their last stronghold had become at Sunderland South Dock, where four of the very last survivors, Nos 65855/11/94/79, all suitably cleaned, stand in the roundhouse prior to their very last day in traffic in the September. Very fortunately, one of these engines, No 65894, survived the scrapyards, thanks to donations made to the NELPG by enthusiasts from all over the UK.

not only in Scotland, but anywhere from Blackpool to Aberdeen and maybe even farther afield.

One of my own favourites were Dundee's North British J37s, which were rostered on freight turns to Montrose. At the sub-shed at Montrose, another J37 was usually out-stationed. Being of wooden construction, this was a little dream of a depot, with its own coaling dock and turntable nearby. The normal duty for the loco was a daily freight turn on the Brechin branch and

the shed was the scene of countless cleaning operations and the subject of numerous stories. On one occasion, the steam-raiser came to work without a box of matches, only to ask us if we had any! On another day, a photographer, Chris Weston, freely admitted that he had cleaned the J37 overnight and, while waiting in his chosen spot on the branch on a hot summer's day, had fallen asleep - only to be awoken by the noise as the loco passed by… and far too late to photograph it!

THE GRAND FINALE OF BRITISH STEAM

Other adventures in 1966, included great times cleaning ex-NER J27s Nos 65842 and 65874 at South Blyth, for the operation of the Woodburn branch in rural Northumberland. Sometimes things would not turn out right, for example, when as usual we only cleaned one side of the engine for the photograph and the driver then forgot to turn the engine! Similarly, we once cleaned Q6 No 63387 at Sunderland, only for it to work just 'engine and van' up Seaton Bank – this was not what we had in mind! Worse though, was an ex-Crosti-boilered 9F cleaned at Leeds Holbeck, whose turn was cancelled altogether and, we being 20 miles away waiting at the lineside, we never knew! This is what it was like in the final year of steam, trying to capture engines we had made respectable – but there was never any absolute guarantee of success. The autumn of 1966 saw a flurry of Scottish Region 'last runs'. First was the last A4, No 60019 Bittern, working between Glasgow and Aberdeen on 3 September, whose buffers I had painted white – the paint still being wet as it left Glasgow! The following month, on 8 October, was the final trip of the Peppercorn A2s. On that occasion, I spent the night on Edinburgh St Margaret's shed cleaning No 60532 Blue Peter and the steam-raiser was so sympathetic to the cause that he allowed me to drive the engine, at 02:00, from the running shed to the coaling plant, prior to departure – I just could not believe it! Later, I photographed it at Shankend on the Waverley Route, but, in true Blue Peter-efficient style, the double chimney was clear - a total contrast to the single-chimney Tudor Minstrel, seen some time earlier over the same route.

On 5 November, I was back in Edinburgh, cleaning the last V2, No 60836, for its final run to Aberdeen and travelled on the train on its unforgettable southbound run. It was so off-beat, but sounded magnificent when climbing out of Montrose and, despite the dubious mechanical condition, it fully completed what was its final official task - before withdrawal. Finally, the last Scottish B1, No 61278, worked over the Waverley Route on 3 December and, super-cleaned, was photographed as it laid a smokescreen over Whitrope Summit in the day's failing light.

1967 was to be the last year of truly main-line steam, but, remarkably, the J37s still held on to the Brechin branch

'TO A DIGNIFIED END'

until as late as March. That year did bring to an end these memorable trips to Scotland, but there were still other places to go. The real highlights by now were in the North East, where the last pre-grouping engines - the old Q6 and J27s - were still working 'bonus turns' from Sunderland South Dock and Hartlepool. Many J27s were cleaned, my hands being dirtied on Nos 65817, 65882, 65879 and 65894. The Q6s were not forgotten, with Sunderland's

No 63395 and Hartlepool's No 63387

ending their working lives immaculate.

I never thought I would ever clean a WD 2-8-0, until, just three days before the end of steam in the North East, the Sunderland roster board said, '90009 coal from Easington to Consett'. Consett? I could not believe it! This would obviously be the last steam to Consett, so, on my own, I cleaned No 90009, to duly photograph her on the stiff 1-in-35 climb at Beamish - with arranged black smoke.

Leeds Holbeck, at this time, still had

three 'Jubilees', No 45593 Kolhapur, No 45562 Alberta and No 45697 Achilles on its allocation. One of these became rostered for the relief 'Thames Clyde Express' on Saturdays throughout the summer and, on every occasion, they were cleaned by enthusiasts on the Friday night before. Upon starting to clean No 45697, when the layers of dirt were removed, the green boiler was found to be unlined, but its tender was lined out, but painted black! This had obviously come from a 'Black Five'.

The end of September saw the cleaning of the last B1, No 61306, at Low Moor, prior to the last Bradford to Leeds working with steam at the head of the 'Yorkshire Pullman'.

Carlisle Kingmoor still had the Britannia Pacifics, which were a fine attraction over Shap - when they could be tracked down. On December Saturday mornings, one of their final workings included the Carlisle to Manchester (Red Bank) empty parcel vans. On three consecutive weekends, the rostered Britannia was cleaned and, on two occasions, photographed climbing to Shap - with steam leaking from everywhere… and in driving rain. Hopeless! The final one we cleaned –

No 70045 Lord Rowallan - was however caught on camera at Low Gill in the Lune Gorge and, at last, the sun shone! Kingmoor's last passenger working of all was, of course, the Carlisle to Blackpool football excursion, when No 70013 Oliver Cromwell was cleaned to perfection on Christmas Day. This occasion did bring to a close the real end of cleaning of express passenger engines in Britain.

In early 1968, with steam now banished from the Northern Fells and,

ABOVE On a perfect sunny morning at Carnforth shed in May 1967, Carlisle Kingmoor's unique Stephenson link motion LMS 'Black Five' No 44767 is cleaned by (L to R) Christopher Weston, Paul Claxton, Dave Gouldthorp and Ian 'Bert' Robb, as well as the photographer, prior to working a Morecambe to Leeds passenger train

entirely by the enthusiasts. After transfer to Carnforth, the last Britannia No 70013 Oliver Cromwell had become a celebrity engine and, now being cleaned just about every weekend, its paintwork was always immaculate.

I did take a week's holiday, concentrating on the final freight workings from Carnforth. There were a few highlights, such as on the Barrow line, with Arnside viaduct, Grange- over-Sands and Kents Bank, where coal, freight and parcels trains still operated. My favourite, however, was the Windermere branch – a line that went to the hills and a goods yard that still had a daily delivery of wagons for the coal merchant. We cleaned Nos 45017 and 45025 at Carnforth.

The Grassington line from Skipton was another branch that saw steam to the very end and No 75034 was once cleaned up at Carnforth for that duty. The loco eventually being loaned to Rose Grove specifically for the purpose, Nos 75019, 75027 and 75048 also came to regularly attain their own super-shine finishes at the latter establishment.

with that, also from the main line, life would no longer be quite the same. I would now be venturing to new parts of the country – in the North West. The year got off to a bright start with several weekends at Buxton cleaning 8Fs in the old LNWR loco shed;

Nos 48775, 48744, 48532 and 48191 being among those to receive the treatment. Unexpectedly, this produced some better than expected results. However, those glorious images of snow and steam hard at work, captured in frosty weather, would provide the very last opportunities to do this with BR steam - it only having months to go before the end.

. Railtours kept the pulse racing and every engine on every railtour was now polished to perfection, usually almost

On one occasion near the very end, 'Black Five' No 45134 had a layover at Kendal goods yard where the front end was quickly cleaned up prior to working back to Carnforth, producing one of my last decent shots of BR steam on freight – the footplate crew even co-operating with the smoke! Cleaning occurred at Kendal and Windermere on other occasions as well.

On 28 July 1968, there was a major session at Rose Grove, cleaning engines for the weekend's railtours. My own contributions were to 8F No 48773 and 'Black Five' No 45156 Ayrshire Yeomanry, on both of which the paint work did come up really well.

It was while on top of the boiler of No 45156 that day, that I noticed a light-blue Morris Minor police car driving right up to where we were working. We feared the worst. Had the shedmaster called in the law to remove the trespassing engine cleaners? Were we all to be 'booked' and fined… on the penultimate weekend of BR steam? I then could not believe my eyes, as the two policemen got out of the car to just stand and watch, but taking no action whatsoever! Realising this was a

LEFT Having been cleaned every Friday evening by enthusiasts at Leeds Holbeck shed, the last three active Jubilees – Nos 45593 Kolhapur, 45697 Achilles and 45562 Alberta - pose in the roundhouse in August 1967. Every Saturday throughout the summer of 1967, one of these magnificent engines worked over the Settle and Carlisle line on the relief 'Thames Clyde Express'

major photographic opportunity in the history of steam (!), I carefully walked behind the policemen (not that I had done this before, you understand) to take a picture of them watching us - the last engine cleaners on BR – cleaning engines. They never did realise!

So, upon reflection, what we did all those years ago in trying to photograph the last engines of BR was, for those involved, great fun, working with good company. From my first engine-cleaning experience with A4 No 60027 Merlin at Perth, to the last time with No 70013 Oliver Cromwell at Lostock Hall on 4 August 1968, there are a thousand happy memories in between.

Although what we accomplished was frequently without permission, on shed most of us were never challenged for trespassing. We possessed neither overalls nor safety boots, and no-one ever showed us the correct methods for climbing onto boilers, or onto the tops of tenders, but, despite this, no-one ever got hurt. More importantly, perhaps, we had no idea of what was supposed to be the proper method to clean engines, but, somehow, we did manage it, and managed it very well.

So what was left behind for us all

today? Certainly, countless memorable photographs exist of our immaculate engines, of which only a few can be shown here, but there is something far more fundamental that has survived. For those involved in working so close to steam, many of us dearly wished that we could have saved all of those locomotives that we took such great pains to work upon.

My final photograph in this chapter, taken at the conclusion of the very last cleaning session at Lostock Hall, depicts some of our youthful group, posing on Lostock Hall's 8F No 48476 – the very last engine cleaners on BR. Among that gathering are faces that many readers may recognise today as later going on to assume major roles in the steam preservation movement. Some helped the NYMR or the Severn Valley. Others assisted in the fund-raising for and purchase of engines from BR by NELPG. Yet others later went on to rescue locomotives from Barry scrapyard. Some became volunteer firemen, or engine drivers, while others became engineers, involved in the restoration of steam engines to working order. One or two others even ended up in BR management roles.

Many of those depicted in that

photograph have been in the steam preservation movement for a lifetime and I sincerely believe that, for them, it may very well all have started with cleaning the last engines on BR. A great deal more than just old photographs remains from those activities of 40 years ago and more. Those engine-cleaning pursuits sowed some of the seeds for the enthusiasm that has help shape, in no small way, the preservation movement that we know so well today.

LEFT At the conclusion of the final engine cleaning session of 3-4 August 1968, some of those involved pose on 8F 2-8-0 No 48476 at Lostock Hall shed. They are left to right on the running plate – Bob Clarke, Geoff Simpson, John Barnes, Dave Lacey, Dave Wilkinson, the late Ken Groundwater and Ian Krause... and below left to right – Jim Bodfish, Pete Proud, Kev Gould, Dave Gouldthorp, Tony Bending, Barry Buckfield, Neville Stead, Dave Williams and Mick York. It should be noted that many of those named, even in 1968, were already involved in the steam preservation movement and were later instrumental in shaping the railway preservation movement we all know so well today.

Chapter 4

Never Again!

The trials and tribulations of steam photography in the 1960s

Railway photography, to me, was more of a way of life than a hobby. It began early in 1961, at a time when I chased trains on a push-bike. Photographically speaking, the first 12 months weren't up to much - a sort of trial and error period. However, cycle trips became longer and faster particularly when, in 1963, I chased LNWR 'Super D' 0-8-0 No 49361 around Birmingham on an SLS special, photographing it in no fewer than eight different locations.

On 3 March 1963, when the country was still in the depths of the 'Big Freeze', I left Coventry on that bicycle at 02:00 for Aylesbury. It was the last day of steam-hauled local passenger services on the Great Central and I obtained photographs at every station from Aylesbury (at first light) to Charwelton (at dusk) in the one day. Every few miles, I had to get off and sprint some distance, in an effort to keep my circulation going. Even so, my hands and feet stayed completely numb, but I am sure it was worth the effort!

My first Pentax SLR camera came on the scene in April 1963; its first outing being to Hatton Bank to photograph all 12 FA Cup semi-final specials on the occasion of Southampton's visit to Villa Park. The sight of Bulleid Pacifics, in addition to the regular diet of Castles and Halls, made quite a spectacle. Before the arrival of the Pentax, all my work was done on colour film. Initially

The 'MNA', an acronym for the 'Master Neverers Association', was an organisation founded upon a common desire to travel by train, while avoiding paying for the privilege. Its members also cleaned steam engines in their spare time and countless enthusiasts in the mid-1960s came to be in the debt of this group of young men, in recognition for those sterling efforts so selflessly extended to permit steam to die with at least some dignity. In the period in which the group flourished, between the mid-1960s and that final dramatic finalé at Lostock Hall on 4 August 1968 (when 13 engines were cleaned in one final, marathon, overnight session), there was a feeling of almost Masonic brotherhood about the organisation. The unspoken and unopposed leader was Paul Riley, who went on to create what is arguably one of the most exciting steam photographic collections of the period. Attempts to obtain the ultimate 'master-shot' were never going to be easy and usually required considerable effort, often resulting in little reward.

Raw steam power at its finest! Greenholme, December 1967. In the failing light of a winter's afternoon, during the final week of steam over Shap Fell, a northbound fitted-freight hauled by a Stanier 'Black Five' is assisted to the summit by one of Tebay shed's Standard 4MT 4-6-0s.

ABOVE Paul Riley (left) with fellow engine cleaners Dave Gouldthorp and Tim Stephens on 65842 at Woodburn, September 1966

Pacific No 60007 Sir Nigel Gresley on an RCTS special to Edinburgh, but, as it turned out, the picture was to be one of the worst I ever took on the line. The position I chose was just north of Riccarton Junction and, being some ten miles up the l-in-70 from Newcastleton, I anticipated that it would be struggling with 12 bogies (450 tons) behind the tender. There was even a V2 on standby at Riccarton, but in the event, No 60007 broke all records, clearing Whitrope summit at 38mph, with a clear chimney.

During subsequent visits to the Waverley Route, to photograph the only four steam workings per day, I became acquainted with a crowd of 'gentlemen' from the Midlands and, one weekend in the winter of 1965, six of us met up at Crewe. Taking the overnight Birmingham-Glasgow train as far as Carlisle, we transferred to the 04:45 to Edinburgh, as far as Hawick. Arriving in 20 degrees of frost, we then walked the 18-odd miles back to Steele Road and returned in the early hours of Sunday morning replete with only one shot. This was of a V2 at Shankend with the 08:06 Millerhill-Carlisle freight. Surprisingly, everyone was happy, perhaps due to the unsurpassed peace and

using Perutz, I switched to Agfa CT18, before deciding upon Kodachrome II for the last 18 months of steam. For my black and white photography, I mainly used Kodak Plus-X, but when conditions demanded I used Tri-X and Pan-X.

Saturday 26 September 1964, was the date of my first of many pilgrimages to the Waverley Route. The trip was basically to photograph Gresley A4 class

NEVER AGAIN!

beauty of the Border Country in winter which almost made the photography a secondary exercise.

During the summer of 1964, I travelled to Beattock, on the last day of the Glasgow Fairs Holiday, to photograph the returning specials from Blackpool and Morecambe, always an interesting affair, as Carlisle Kingmoor was invariably short of locomotives. I left Carlisle on one of those specials, after first checking with the crew that they would be taking assistance up the bank. At Beattock, I transferred from train to banker, for a lift to the summit and then started to walk back down the bank. Before first light (a fortnight at f2 exposure!), A2 Pacific No 60535 Hornet's Beauty went up the bank, to be followed by Stanier Pacific No 46255 City of Hereford.

After a good day, photographing a varied assortment of motive power, I waited at Beattock station for a southbound train and was not disappointed when No 46235 City of Birmingham drew into the platform. To my amazement, the Duchess was not taken off at Carlisle and continued south to Crewe. Having travelled back behind steam from Beattock, I was determined to

Unquestionably one of the finest steam action photographs taken in the Lune Gorge. On 25 February 1967, Stanier Jubilee 4-6-0 No 45562 Alberta creates an almost mystic effect in taking on slightly more than a full load of water as it thunders over Dillicar Troughs with the 'Border Countryman' railtour from Leeds to Beattock. Some slight adjustments (allegedly) having been made by the photographer to the water level in the troughs (a somewhat lower level by that time having been established for diesels with steam-heating boilers), the fireman had clearly not anticipated such an unexpected bonus! It, perhaps, goes without saying that Mr Riley's public-spirited efforts would not have been appreciated by any 'window-hangers' in the leading coach!

Express power at rest! A nocturnal interlude at Leeds Holbeck depot in Summer 1967. Having been polished to perfection by the MNA, two of the three remaining members of the Jubilee class 4-6-0, Nos 45562 Alberta and 45593 Kolhapur, await their day's duties, which will include working a couple of summer Saturday reliefs over the Settle & Carlisle line.

continue behind steam to either Rugby or Birmingham - no matter how long it took! Six hours later, my prayers were answered in the form of another Duchess, this time

No 46240 City of Coventry. The engine took over the relief 'Irish Mail', which departed some 40 minutes late with 14 bogies behind the tender and Riley on the footplate trying his hand at firing. Having uprated a roll of Tri-X to 3200ASA and still only managing to get an exposure of a thirtieth of a second at f2, I managed a shot of the speedometer

reading 90-plus mph, quite an achievement on a locomotive footplate!

The year of 1965 was a very eventful one in Scotland. I had three separate weeks' holiday to concentrate on the Glasgow-Aberdeen route. Daytime was spent taking photographs, usually finishing at Perth in time to catch the southbound 'West Coast Postal', which continued to Stirling, before the passenger Glasgow portion was split. The first night that I travelled on this train, I got chatting to the Carstairs crew, who adopted me as fireman as far as

Stirling, following which I continued to Glasgow, where I picked up the 23:00 to Aberdeen. This was a regular A4 turn and, by 'kipping on the cushions', I arrived at 03:00 in time to go down to the fish market for breakfast. These arrangements continued for most of that week and, occasionally, I would fire the A4 back to Aberdeen. One night, while noshing an Angus steak butty in Perth refreshment rooms, the fireman of the 20:25 'Postal' entered in a fuming temper and threw his gloves at me, uttering obscenities about a Britannia (although that wasn't what he called

it!) that wouldn't steam. I took the hint and, as it was 20:00, I had 25 minutes to sort it out. I first tried the pricker, but the clinker was absolutely solid. So, all I could do was to build up the fire very carefully, but at 20:25, only 160psi showed on the gauge. The driver opened the regulator fully, allowing

No 70041 Sir John Moore to slip violently (a last resort to break up the fire), but, after firing steadily to Gleneagles, there was still only 160psi on the gauge. This remained constant to Stirling, where the idle fireman talked me into carrying on to Carstairs. Here, he was relieved by the Carstairs crew, who were equally happy to let me continue to Carlisle and where we arrived at midnight with Riley completely knackered. However, after a wash and breakfast in the railwaymen's bothy, I boarded the 02:25 to Perth behind another Britannia, No 70048 The Territorial Army 1908-1958. By

NEVER AGAIN!

Beattock, I was back on the footplate back to Perth, where I took a well-earned couple of hours 'kip' in the three-star 'ECS Hotel'.

It was during this same week, while busy working Hilton Junction box, that I met Maurice Burns, just as A4 No 60027 Merlin came past with the 10:15 ex-Edinburgh. Both Maurice and I decided to go round to Perth MPD to ascertain the return working. When questioned, the foreman replied that it would be returning to Edinburgh at 14:55. Just as we were about to go off shed and back up the line, we looked at No 60027, then at each other, realising that it was quite the filthiest A4 that we had ever seen. We decided it could do with cleaning. Tongue-in-cheek, we returned to the foreman and asked if we could clean it. His reply was that he hadn't any cleaners on shed. To this, we said again that WE would clean it. Very mildly and half-heartedly, he said that we couldn't do that. Not getting the inevitable marching orders, we decided to hunt round for some cotton waste and paraffin. Working very fast, we had the engine clean in no time, but hit problems with the tender. A ladder was needed, so I slipped back into the gloom of the shed and laid my hands on one. Heading back to the yard and

No 60027, I was spotted by the foreman. After all, I was a bit conspicuous with a damned great ladder over my shoulder. Carrying on, I sensed I was being followed, all the time fearing the big crunch and having to photograph a clean locomotive and dirty tender. By the time that he had caught up with me, I had the ladder up on the tender and was going like mad with the cotton waste. To our amazement, he stood watching with his hands behind his back and mouth wide open.

Eventually, the silence broke: "Ach, a've noo ever seen anything like it in 40 years of service!" He then insisted on being photographed with us and No 60027! (See previous chapter) Even so, the final photograph at Glenfarg was a dead loss - but the cleaning session was very significant in being the first of a very long line of similar tasks. This procedure spread so rapidly and with such keen interest that crowds of us would leave our homes on Friday evenings to clean up anything from the Lymington branch engine to A4s at Aberdeen (Ferryhill).

In 1965, BR approached me for the use of some of my photographs taken on the West Highland line for a Highland Railway exhibition in Inverness - and asked me to name my own price. I asked for 30/- (£1.50)... and a bit of co-operation regarding LNER A2 No 60530 Sayajirao of Dundee (62B). These single-chimney A2s had haunted me and I couldn't get one working on an ordinary passenger train. This was annoying, particularly after seeing all the WJV Anderson masterpieces - yes, I was jealous! My request was that No 60530 should be rostered to work the 10:15 Dundee-Glasgow and the 18:15 return for one week, commencing 30 August. To this, BR agreed in part, namely to roster it for the Monday only. As Sundays were fairly quiet in Scotland, Dave Gouldthorp and I decided to spend the afternoon cleaning No 60530 on Dundee MPD. Unfortunately, we hadn't allowed for the temperament of the shed foreman, who just wouldn't hear of us cleaning one of HIS engines. Not to be outdone, we crept back at 02:00 and spent three hours cleaning the loco, until you could have eaten your dinner off the top of the boiler! Next, it was off to Auchterarder for the outward journey

LEFT Such is the sedate progress of this heavy train, that No 48448 is seen again a mile or so further on from the picture at the foot of the page, this time leaving Holme Tunnel and within yards of Copy Pit Summit, where brakes will be pinned down for the switchback descent to Hall Royd Junction, Todmorden

Having worked a train of empties earlier in the day over to Healey Mills Yard, No 48448 now returns home with a Healey Mills to Wyre Dock load of coal. On a line that even today continues to produce seemingly endless new photo opportunities on its climb from Todmorden to Copy Pit summit, the 8F is seen winding its way through the rooftops on the reverse curves near Portsmouth.

and to Dunblane for the return. As BR had informed me that it was for one day only, we took off for Ayrshire and the Fowler 'Crabs' on the Tuesday, only to find on our return to Glasgow that No 60530 had worked the same turn again. Back to Dundee we went, to check the roster board for the Wednesday which read '10.15am Glasgow - 44718'. During the wee hours this mysteriously became '10.15 am Glasgow - 60530' !

As luck would have it, we just happened to be at Hilton Junction to photograph the outward journey and St Rollox for the return. Although Monday evening's shot was useless, the other three were quite acceptable - all this in just three days… after three years of trying.

In April 1967, I procured a provisional driving licence and, after three or four hours' tuition, I purchased a beat-up Vauxhall Wyvern for £40. The first jaunt, to Birkenhead, was obviously a trial and error affair, although the normally steel nerves of my passengers began to soften well before we got back to Birmingham.

After only a couple of months, the old Vauxhall began to break up - liter¹ ally. The Buxton-Glossop road claimed the front bumper and the back one disappeared while chasing a special on the Southern near Andover. The last trip with it was certainly the most interesting. With the usual complement of five in the car, we chased a Stanier Class 5 up Shap, from Tebay, and when cornering fairly hard, it started to handle very strangely. Upon investigation (naturally, after the shot) we discovered that a 2ft length of leaf spring had come through the boot. The following day, we continued to Berwick to see preserved A4 No 4498 Sir Nigel Gresley and, upon checking the oil and water levels, I noticed that the engine had developed a ten-degree list to one side (due to shattered engine mountings). This really put the wind up me, to the extent of imposing a 30mph speed limit for the rest of the trip, for fear of having a 1500cc engine on our laps. Having taken the shot of No 4498 on Cockburnspath Bank, we commenced the return journey from Grantshouse to Coventry. Thirteen hours of solid driving later, with stops only for black coffee, it was straight into work - and

they called this enjoyment!

The next arrival on the scene was a beautiful blue 12-year-old Mk 1 Ford Zephyr, which was to outlast BR steam - just. Eighteen months and 60,000 miles takes some stamina, especially for a 12-year-old. It was with this motor that I discovered radial tyres, especially after getting only 6000 miles from a set of cross-plies. This change to radials definitely increased consumption - shots per mile that is!

On Monday 5 February 1968, it snowed heavily and the forecast was for more, so I thought conditions would be

BELOW Snaking round the reverse curves between Cornholme and Portsmouth, 8F 2-8-0 No 48247 climbs to Copy Pit summit with a Healey Mills to Wyre Dock coal train. Banking assistance at the rear is provided by sister engine number No 48257, which, as yet, is still out of sight. 24 February 1968

NEVER AGAIN!

RIGHT On the very last day of steam, 2 March 1968, Stanier 8F 2-8-0 No 48744 has been rostered to work a stone train up the Hindlow branch to Briggs Sidings As this duty produced the last engine to be booked off Buxton shed in revenue-earning service and, having been specially cleaned the previous night, it is now the centre of attention for railway men and enthusiasts alike as it is turned to work chimney-first up the hill out of town

perfect for the Buxton area with 8Fs off Gowhole and working up to Chinley and Chapel-en-le-Frith. So, with two 1cwt iron castings (borrowed from work) and two large shovels, (these would be well used before the day was out) in the boot, and with two passengers on the back seat, we left Coventry at 05:00 for a trip which usually takes an hour and a half. It soon became evident that things were not going to be easy, with the M6 looking more like a battlefield than a motorway. Vehicles were abandoned everywhere - not only on the hard shoulder, but over all six lanes as well. I managed to pick my way through these and got to Macclesfield at 07:00, although the town had, officially, been cut-off since midnight.

The snow was still falling, but after much discussion we decided to attempt to reach Gowhole via Whaley Bridge. We soon started to encounter problems on the climb out of Macclesfield, as the route was up a l-in-10 out of the town. Nevertheless, I managed to pass everything that was stuck, including a milk float with snow-chains. At the top of the hill, with snow drifting to depths of over 4ft in places, two lorries had collided and closed the road, so we had to turn back and try another way out. This time, we tried the direct road to Buxton (the A537) known locally as the 'Cat & Fiddle Road', after the pub high on the moors and much renowned in this type of weather - but I'd never heard of it - then. I soon learned!

The first few miles were relatively easy, but then we hit snow drifts up to 8ft deep. I soon discovered the only way of continuing was to hit the drifts at 30-40mph, first knocking a hole in them and, of course, getting stuck, before reversing about 200 yards and blasting through the gap. Inevitably, the car eventually became embedded, so at that point the shovels came out and we started digging. This process continued for over an hour, with our making only minimal progress, probably about two miles in that time.

We were now heading into the country, with little sign of habitation, and from here the rate of progress was very slow and strenuous. It must have been sheer lunacy, but we pushed on... until it happened. I completely missed a Y-junction and embedded the motor in 4ft of snow. I had become almost completely buried in a particularly deep drift, with the car partly off the road,

when out of the blizzard came two large headlights. It was a huge snowplough, which stopped just short of our car. The driver got out of the cab, came over to us and asked where we were heading. "Buxton," was our reply, to which his response was, "Are you crazy? This road's been closed for the last 24 hours!" It was at this point that we decided to dig the car out, turn it round, and head back to Macclesfield, trailing the snowplough.

Back in the café, we recovered from the hypothermia/exhaustion with mugs of hot tea, and then referred to the map to plan our next move. We decided that a safer bet would be to head north on the A523 and then take the A6 south of Stockport. This we managed to do,

without too much bother, although a number of trees had been brought down across the A6 south of Chapel-en-le-Frith, but by this time the route had been cleared for traffic.

We finally arrived in Buxton sometime in the early afternoon, and headed straight for the sheds. I remember attempting to drive down an alleyway on the approach to the MPD, but the car became stuck in another snowdrift. "You go and see what's working and I'll dig the car out," I said to Allan Stewart, so he headed away from the car and up a banking, only to discover the sheds standing in an oasis of undisturbed snow. It was pretty obvious that no engines had moved that day. Determined to find the answer, Allan stumbled across the hidden tracks and into the building. At

the shed foreman's office, he politely asked, "What engines will be working today?" - only to be met with the reply: "You don't think we'd send engines out in this weather, do you?" Allan headed back to the car to give me the bad news and, in fact, we both then had a good laugh at the foreman's rhetoric!

After that, there was only one place to go and that was to the local alehouse, before the return journey to Coventry, which was a little easier and did involve no shovelling. Nine 8Fs and one 'Black Five' were on shed that day and we didn't get a single photo - even of RDU 290 stuck in the drifts!

The following Saturday, we were off up to Buxton again, with another 05:00am start. We made it this time and managed to photograph steam in the last of the clearing snow.

Yes, RDU 290 certainly did herself justice and ended her life in a blaze of glory. On Boxing Day 1967, with new engine just run-in and tuned to perfection, we took off for Shap with five for Britannia No 70013 Oliver Cromwell on a football special to Blackpool.

We arrived at Strickland Woods in frosty, foggy weather, but as No 70013 appeared, the sun broke through, just like magic and, contrary to expectations, stayed out all day. From Strickland to Shap Summit, we caught the train at six different locations and then decided to continue chasing to Preston, this with the help of 105mph from RDU 290.

On the M6 we overtook the train and then, from 90mph to a dead stand on the hard shoulder, we halted under a bridge with the car-bonnet up, scrambling up onto the bridge to shoot 70013. Then it was back to the car to slam the bonnet shut, with 37 shots of Oliver Cromwell in the bag... all in immaculate condition and ideal weather!

After all these years, there is still a weekend in August when we all get together at The Station Inn at Ribblehead. After drinking to all hours and singing all those educational rugby songs, the following morning sees us collecting all the stragglers - who have the knack of ending up anything up to two miles away from everyone else. This annual reunion is now the high point of the year and will continue, I am convinced, until the last one of us has drawn his last breath!

Paul Riley (1945 to 1976)

LEFT Trafford Park MPD in early 1968. The former 'joint' depot was particularly interesting for the variety of engines, including Great Central and Midland types until the end of the 1950s, augmented briefly by some of Great Northern and even of Great Eastern origin. Here, Stanier 8F No 48356 pokes its nose out from under a roof that has seen much better days. With a continuing lack of maintenance to the structure, most of the remainder of the roof had already been removed altogether

Chapter 5

Peak steam farewell

The last winter of steam in Derbyshire

During the first two months of 1968, the attention of most photographers had transferred from the now steamless Shap and Ais Gill to an area south-east of Manchester, where steam was still employed on freight duties. Working along part of the Midland Railway's highly scenic Manchester to Derby main line, through the Derbyshire Peak District, steam still handled minerals traffic from the Manchester area to Buxton and to large lime-works complexes around Peak Forest.

During the course of several successive weekends, and with snow often heavy on the ground, a series of apparently never-ending freights, hauled by specially cleaned 8Fs 'performed to the gallery' in the area between Gowhole Yard and Dove Holes Tunnel.

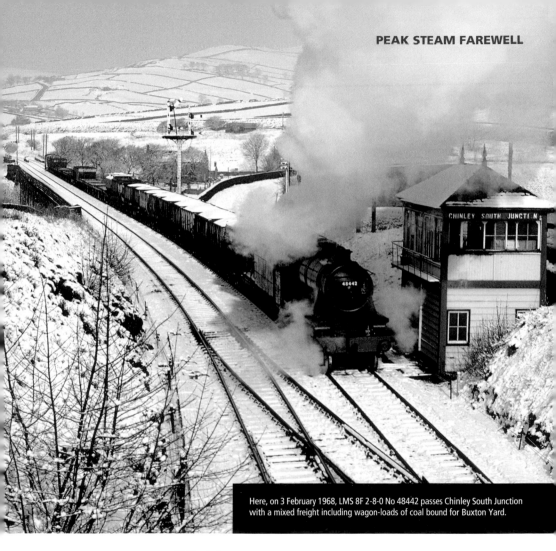

Here, on 3 February 1968, LMS 8F 2-8-0 No 48442 passes Chinley South Junction with a mixed freight including wagon-loads of coal bound for Buxton Yard.

Always a location popular with photographers is Chinley North Junction. The home signal is pulled off, permitting 8F 2-8-0 No 48744 to cross over the junction to head a train of 16-ton mineral wagons up the former Midland main line towards Peak Forest. January 1968.

There is no doubt as to the location of this photograph! Heading for Buxton, 8F 2-8-0 No 48442 passes over the lofty viaduct forming Chinley North curve, with a freight working bound for Buxton Yard on 3 February 1968.

In early 1968, operational difficulties became compounded, when problems in Dove Holes Tunnel dictated that single-line working had to be initiated for weeks on end, while engineering work continued. This meant that up trains had to reverse onto the down line at Chapel-en-le-Frith, in order to work 'wrong-line' as far as Peak Forest, this, at times, producing inevitable bottle-necks to traffic. At nearly 1000ft above sea level and at the summit of a long climb at 1-in-90, 8F 2-8-0 No 48191 emerges from the 2984 yards-long Dove Holes Tunnel with a Gowhole Yard to Buxton train of mineral empties in February 1968.

Buxton shed's 8F 2-8-0 No 48465 shunts loaded coal wagons in the sidings adjacent to the quarry of the Buxton Lime Company (now RMC Roadstone) at Peak Forest. Although the quarry still despatches stone by rail today, most of the buildings depicted in this January 1968 view have since disappeared.

On 17 February 1968, 8F 2-8-0s Nos 48775 and 48424 double-head a heavy rock train past Peak Forest summit, bound for Port Talbot in South Wales. It will be noticed that No 48775 still possesses its WD-type top-feed and that No 48424 has a larger than normal vacuum ejector on the side of the boiler.

The Torrs at New Mills is a dramatic gorge, above which the town perches and along the bottom of which lie 18th century mills and weirs on the River Goyt. Here, in early 1968, Edge Hill's 8F 2-8-0 No 48056 heads a Gowhole Yard to Garston freight towards New Mills Central Station.

Ashwood Dale is a spectacularly narrow deep-cut and tree-lined valley just outside Buxton. Here, Stanier 8F 2-8-0 No 48191 threads one of the most scenic sections, past Lovers Leap, with a Gowhole to Buxton freight in February 1968.

Chapter 6

Springtime 1968
Everyday steam around the north west

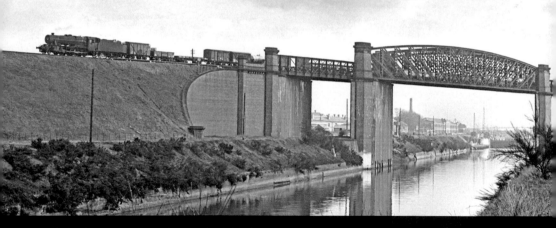

Latchford Viaduct was opened on 8 July 1893 and carried the former LNWR Stockport to Warrington line over the Manchester Ship Canal. It has a span of 250ft and weighs more than 1200 tonnes. Although the structure still survives today, its closure to rail traffic was due in no small part to its poor condition - the line seeing its last passengers in 1962, but continuing to carry some freight until July 1985. Here, in January 1968, Speke Junction's Stanier 8F No 48168 heads a Garston-bound fitted goods.

badly leaking steam locomotives, grimy rolling stock, BRUTE trolleys, mailbags lying unattended on station platforms... and duffel bags? All integral components of the typical 1960s steam scene and all now vanished with nary a trace. A Manchester engine for the whole of its life, but now relegated to duties which are a far cry from when It arrived brand new at Patricroft shed 20 years previously, the now Newton Heath-allocated No 45420 is Manchester Victoria station pilot on 30 March 1968. The loco is stood in the celebrated Platform 11 which, at 2194ft, was the longest platform in the UK.

Another picture taken on 30 March 1968. In between other duties, station pilot No 45420 takes on water from a column at the south end of Platform 17. Notice the high-level shut-off valve, enabling the fireman to monitor the water supply more accurately from the tender-top. The driver stands on the platform ready to pull the arm away from the tender, but notice also that he stands well clear from any possibility of a soaking!

THE GRAND FINALE OF BRITISH STEAM

Conveying coal for Micklehurst Power Station, Stockport Edgeley's Stanier 8F 2-8-0 No 48549 departs from Stalybridge, along the truncated spur of the former Micklehurst Loop to Diggle, with 'Target 27', the 06:10 from Guide Bridge to Staley & Millbrook. Both the loop line and the power station are now long demolished

High above the rooftops of Bolton, 'Black Five' No 45312 crosses the viaduct carrying the Blackburn line out of town, in the process of working between Horwich and Halliwell on Bolton shed's Turn No 11, which supplies the motive power for 'No 212 Target'. Upon arrival at Halliwell, No 45312 will then return tender-first with a load of wagons destined for Moston Sidings.

The Torrs at New Mills is a dramatic gorge, above which the town perches and along the bottom of which lie 18th century mills and weirs on the River Goyt. Here, in early 1968, Edge Hill's 8F 2-8-0 No 48056 heads a Gowhole Yard to Garston freight towards New Mills Central Station.

With a heavy coal train, banked in the rear by No 48519, Stanier 8F No 48410 slogs past Portsmouth and up the last half-mile to Copy Pit Summit, on 18 May 1968. This particular engine was a former Western Region locomotive, having spent several years allocated to Old Oak Common and is easily distinguished by its different design of vacuum ejector.

8P19, the 12:00 Burnley Central to Burn Naze, was a regular coal train working into the Fylde. On 24 April 1968, 8F No 48400 speeds past Weeton with a load of 22-ton twin-doored wagons, specifically used on this turn.

The last duties for the remaining Ivatt 4MT 2-6-0s – all based at Lostock Hall in 1968 – mainly consisted of station pilot duties at Preston Station. On 12 April 1968, No 43027 is seen awaiting its next task in the sidings between the old Platforms 2 and 3.

Until the closure of Newton Heath depot at the end of June, one of the few daytime steam workings over the Bolton – Blackburn line in 1968 was 5J13, the 17:05 (SX) Burnley Central to Moston fitted freight. This picture, taken shortly before steam finished on the working, depicts an unidentified 'Black Five' heading downhill over Entwistle Viaduct. With gradually encroaching forestation, views of the viaduct like this one are no longer possible.

Chapter 7

Steaming into the Dales
The last steam branch line

I suppose that it must have been the prospect of a journey for the first time in my life, actually being hauled by a London & North Western Railway locomotive, that was, very indirectly, the innocent cause of my first introduction to the Grassington Branch.

Along with the 'Lanky' Class As, the LNW 'Super D's occupy a major proportion of the surviving train-spotting memories of my earlier youth. In the late 1950s, these two types were synonymous with the contemporary goods yard scene in the Preston area, they were everywhere! I recall being absolutely fascinated watching one after another 0-8-0 emerging from underneath the supporting gantry of Preston's No 2A signalbox, at the head of heavy freight trains, appearing literally to have surfaced from the bowels of the earth, as they roared up the last few yards of that fearsome 1-in-29 gradient from Preston Docks, and invariably being banked at the rear by other members of the class.

With the burning-down and subsequent closure of Preston MPD in June 1960, although much of the allocation was transferred to Lostock Hall, it became only too apparent, even to the casual observer, that the latter establishment was a bastion of all things L&Y and such 'intruders' were apparently unwelcome, any such being fairly rapidly banished to the nearest surviving 'Wessy' establishments to the north and south and where crews were more accustomed to their sometimes temperamental handling traits.

A hive of industry amid the rolling fields of the Yorkshire Dales. On 1 June 1968, a very nicely polished Standard 4MT No 75019 (notice the burnished brass cab spectacles) pulls away from Spencers Sidings with a full load of ballast wagons destined for any one of a dozen destinations around the North West.

Many of the 0-8-0s damaged in the fire, in fact, did not see service again, being destined to storage for many years in the roofless shell of the shed building and the last few working examples from that time onwards coming to be seen on only exceptionally rare occasions. So scarce in fact, were they, that by mid-1962, I actually thought they had all fin-ished in the North West. Nevertheless, it was at that time that a quite unexpected opportunity presented itself, which appeared to be far too good to miss out upon. Through the grapevine, I came to learn of a forthcoming railtour being planned to run in my locality and, not only was a 'Super D' booked to work one of the stages of this but, for

depart from a local branch terminus that, although within easy walking distance of my home, was one at which I had not observed more than one or two trains in my whole lifetime, let alone a full-blown real passenger train! Indeed, Preston (Fishergate Hill) had despatched its last regular passenger workings to Southport over 60 years previously. Absolutely the last fare-paying passengers had crossed its threshold way back in 1951, descending from one or two of the intentionally diverted specials associated with that frenetic excursion traffic during the Preston Guild Week, occurring to 'gridlock' proportions every 20 years. Now known as 'West Lancs Goods', the branch terminus had been reduced in status to the level of receiving but a single daily trip working from a nearby yard, this supplying a cattle foods supply depot based in the old station building.

lucky passengers, there were numerous other equally enticing delights in store. The adventurous itinerary promised the chance to venture upon many lines that, even then, had not seen a passenger train for many a year.

The 'icing on the cake' for me, however, was the chance to be able to

And so it came to pass that, one evening, a friend and I cycled round to the address given on the tour booking form, which turned out to be the home of the secretary of the RCTS (Lancs & North West Branch), to each hand over the £1 or so necessary to purchase tickets.

It was Springs Branch's still-surviving No 49451, which permitted me to achieve both of the afore-ascribed ambitions and I do recall that the loco was sent to Lostock Hall shed a few days prior to the tour, 'for cleaning' – a duty in which my friend and I volunteered to assist. Indeed, for me, that exercise proved to be another personal 'first' and, given what was to transpire in years to come, probably the single major incentive in persuading me that

steam should be allowed to die with some dignity – at least in my photographs!

Although the trip had been entitled the 'Mid Lancs Railtour', this was evidently somewhat of a misnomer, for both the itinerary notes and my Ian Allan Pre-Grouping Atlas & Gazetteer clearly confirmed that, apart from some ingeniously organised gyrations around Lancashire, we were also to delve deep into the Yorkshire Dales, indeed reaching as far as a place called Grassington & Threshfield, of which I then knew nothing.

Well, on 22 September 1962, we set out on our journey of discovery and, after accomplishing a complete 360-degree circle via Lostock Hall, passed through the 'other' Preston Station, before again diving off the main line almost immediately in order to traverse the entire length of the now long-closed Longridge Branch. Soon to be re-engined with Fleetwood shed's far speedier Hughes-Fowler 'Crab' 2-6-0 No 42844, this capably driven by Lostock

FAR LEFT Rylstone Crossing is where once the only intermediate station on the branch, Rylstone (for Cracoe), had stood. Two tall wooden-posted lower quadrant signals protecting the roadway, controlled by a ground-frame in a hut nearby, the gates here have to be operated by the train crew. No 75019 has just arrived and awaits the guard to undertake this task. 1 June 1968

LEFT Standard 4MT 4-6-0 No 75048 exits the 219 yards-long Haw Bank Tunnel, on the approach to Skipton, in April 1968. Although trains on the line to Ilkley have ended three years previously, double-track still survives at this stage as far as Embsay Junction

On 31 May 1968, the final steam freight working of all ran over part of the Settle & Carlisle line. No 75019 worked a 'ballast' from Spencers Sidings to Appleby, in the event coming to be 'looped' at Settle Jct, Horton-in-Ribblesdale, Ribblehead and Blea Moor, much to the delight of the few car-borne photographers 'in-the-know'. This almost unreported working, quite amazingly, had occurred five months after the closure of Kingmoor shed to steam! Here, the train is seen crossing the viaduct at Gargrave.

Hall's Terry Campbell, we then headed straight for East Lancs territory, via a final trip (for most of us) around the Great Harwood Loop, before No 42844 handed over to Skipton's Standard 2MT No 78036, to transport us down the short branch from Earby to Barnoldswick. Returning to Earby once more, we regained No 42844, to again delve even further eastwards, and towards Skipton, where we ran straight into the Ilkley line platforms.

Forging away from Platform 5, the driver opened the regulator wide to begin the stiff climb towards Embsay Junction, No 42844 barking aggressively as we crossed over the Midland main line to Leeds and we disappeared into the stygian gloom of Haw Bank Tunnel. Swirling clouds of sulphurous smoke darted in and out of the carriage windows in the darkness, before suddenly dissipating as we emerged to survey the stupendous views of the rolling Dales now unfolding. The signalman at Embsay Junction was waiting for us and had already descended his steps in order to hand over the tablet for the single-line beyond.

We were now into North Eastern Region territory and, with double-tracks at that time still continuing onwards towards Bolton Abbey and Ilkley, we branched-off to the left. The Ilkley and Arthington routes were to witness their final trains some four years later, with last rites being performed by Neville Hill DMUs during a day, as I recall (for I was there), of heavy snow showers. However, today, the set of rails we were on were transporting us the 8¼ miles towards our own destination of Grassington & Threshfield. This former Midland Railway terminus had closed to passengers somewhat earlier, indeed as far back as 22 September 1930, although the occasional excursions for hikers (and, indeed, railway enthusiasts) continued to visit the area

until the late 1960s.

Squealing around the tight curves, our five-coach rake of LMS stock made towards the hills, ambling along at a much-reduced pace from that experienced earlier, but it was marvellous to lean out of the window to watch the little farms pass by, with sheep scattering in every direction from our path. Soon we came to Rylstone Crossing, where the gates had to be operated by the train crew. Two tall wooden-posted lower quadrant signals protected the roadway, controlled by a ground-frame in a hut nearby. For the more observant, among the long grass could just be discerned the remains of where once the only intermediate station on the branch, Rylstone (for Cracoe), had stood.

We were on our way again and it wasn't long before the great mass of Swinden Lime Works came into view. Everything hereabouts was covered in lime dust - even the grass in the fields. We continued ever onwards and upwards, then, suddenly and without warning, Grassington & Threshfield station opened out before us. The terminus had been built some distance away from the centre of the village and consisted of a long single platform housing the original low-roofed, wooden buildings, all of which still existed 32 years after the last tickets had been sold from the booking office. The original signalbox, however, was moved from its original location into the yard, ultimately to serve a very different purpose, that to be a mountain-rescue post.

No 42844 ran round its stock in the goods yard and, after photographs had been taken, we were soon on our way once again. The fun was not yet over, for, beyond Blackburn, our final treat lay in the traversing of the old Lancashire Union line to Chorley – another route from which passenger traffic had long evaporated. However, for me, the highlight of the tour had been that ride into the Dales. I vowed to return.

And so it was that, the following May, I stepped down as the only passenger from a DMU in Embsay's platform and, working my way through the country lanes, I eventually found Embsay Jct 'box. The ensuing wait at the lineside for an hour or so eventually provided its just desserts. With dieselisation taking hold in parts of Scotland long before it had in much of the rest of the country, I had just missed the magnificent

K4s working over the Mallaig Road. Another RCTS railtour was now to provide me with a sighting of one, albeit this example being far from its natural home and in a livery that I never knew. Running about half an hour late, the West Riding Branch's 'Dalesman' tour from Bradford eventually hove into view from the Ilkley direction and bound for Grassington & Threshfield.

Being a supporter of all things LMS and the products of Crewe and Horwich, I, nevertheless, had a penchant for the syncopated Gresley three-cylinder beat, ever since the first time that I had heard this wonderful sound. The recently restored LNER K4 2-6-0 No 3442 The Great Marquess (ex-BR No 61994) had been booked to work this special and, as it was also the engine's first outing in preservation, the temptation to see it proved irresistible. Running round its stock at this location (as excursions sometimes did), I was able to gaze upon No 3442 for all of 15 minutes, before it was on its way up the single line. That three-cylinder beat was certainly somewhat alien to the more usual sounds usually emanating hereabouts - whether from sheep or the creations of Henry Fowler!

Although scheduled passenger services had been withdrawn nearly 40 years previously, the branch was to remain Grassington, and limestone traffic from the quarries at Threshfield and Swinden was sufficient to ensure a daily pick-up

steam-worked right until to the end of steam on BR. Coal and cattle-feed were regularly delivered to the goods yard at working from Skipton, this always a 'Derby 4' turn from Skipton shed, until the BR Standard Class 4MTs eventually

took over. 'Derby 4s', or other short wheelbase engines, had always been used, as a consequence of the very short run-round head-shunt at the buffer-stops at Grassington, and except for the odd excursion, when the appearance of a 'Crab' 2-6-0 was not unknown, the branch had never seen anything else.

With the demise of steam gaining pace at other arguably more exotic locations and so much more to do with so little time in which to achieve this, it was to be almost another five years before I was to return. In the meantime, Skipton shed had closed to steam in April 1967 and the majority of its allocation of Standard 4MT 4-6-0s had then been transferred to Carnforth. It was Rose Grove shed, however, that took over the working - which had now become part of its

'No 94 Target;' the engine leaving shed at 06:00 to shunt in Skipton Up Sidings, before departing at 09:35 for Spencer's Sidings, on the branch. Curiously, but quite evidently because Carnforth could better utilise a fleet of Standard 4MTs than 10F (and 10A already maintained a spares stock), the same engines continued to maintain their monopoly on the branch.

Working out of Carnforth, one engine at a time, they ran light to and from Rose Grove - being changed around on a quite frequent basis, with most of the 10A allocation appearing from time to time.

In the final throes of steam working, visiting enthusiasts became familiar with Nos 75019, 75027 and 75048, the final three survivors of the class. No 94 Target was shown in the timetable books as terminating in Skipton Yard at 10:28 - in theory. However, in practice, the trainloads of ballast from the quarry were required to be delivered forwards to a whole variety of locations. These included Blackburn, Bamber Bridge, Kirkham and, in several instances during May and June, as far afield as Kirkby Stephen or Appleby.

That, indeed, was the case on 31 May 1968, a date which effectively witnessed the final steam freight working of all over the Settle & Carlisle line. No 75019, on its 'ballast' to Appleby, came to be 'looped' at Settle Jct, Horton-in-Ribblesdale, Ribblehead and Blea Moor, much to the delight of the few car-borne photographers 'in-the-know'. This almost unreported working, quite amazingly, had occurred five months after the closure of Kingmoor shed to steam and five months after Britannia Pacific No 70045 had passed that way on the last official steam freight southwards.

Carnforth depot continued to provide Rose Grove with Standard 4MTs almost until the very end of steam. The, by now long-dieselised, goods services on the branch were eventually to be withdrawn from 11 August 1969 and from that point forward, the line came to rely entirely upon the lucrative minerals traffic for its survival.

Although Grassington had lost its passenger services back in 1930, the holiday excursion traffic continued for many years afterwards; however at the same time as the goods traffic ceased, the final passenger-carrying train also ran into Grassington & Threshfield station. This excursion, promoted by the then embryo Yorkshire Dales Railway Society, operated some 67 years after the opening of the line and brought to a conclusion the final chapter in the story of trains to Grassington.

The rails were soon dismantled beyond Swinden, but 40 years on from the end of steam, the truncated section to the limestone quarry still thrives.

LEFT The classic, archetypal Settle & Carlisle view. After being 'looped', No 75019 climbs noisily away from Horton-in-Ribblesdale. It was difficult to comprehend that, after this historically significant photograph had been taken, the so-familiar location would no longer regularly echo to the sounds of seemingly endless processions of steam-hauled freights

Chapter 8

Early summer steam specials

On 18 May, the Warwickshire Railway Society operated its 'North Western Steam Tour' from Coventry to Blackpool and Morecambe, the Stockport-Todmorden-Blackburn-Bolton-Preston stage of which was worked in tandem by ex-LMS 'Black Five' No 44949 and Standard 5MT No 73069. The train is seen working up-grade out of Blackburn towards Sough Tunnel, passing Hoddlesden Jct (the former junction of the short single-track branch to Hoddlesden, near Darwen).

On 18 May, the Warwickshire Railway Society operated its 'North Western Steam Tour' from Coventry to Blackpool and Morecambe, the Stockport-Todmorden-Blackburn-Bolton-Preston stage of which was worked in tandem by ex-LMS 'Black Five' No 44949 and Standard 5MT No 73069. The train is seen working up-grade out of Blackburn towards Sough Tunnel, passing Hoddlesden Jct (the former junction of the short single-track branch to Hoddlesden, near Darwen).

On 9 June 1968 it was the turn of the London Midland Region to utilise No 70013 on a railtour. Hauling the 'Midland Line Centenary Special' from St Pancras, on its final stage from Derby to Manchester Victoria via Matlock, the special is seen here leaving Litton Tunnel midway on the 1-in-100 climb from Monsal Dale to Millers Dale.

THE GRAND FINALE OF BRITISH STEAM

The 'Midland Line Centenary Special passes Millers Dale Junction. No 70013 Oliver Cromwell was the last steam locomotive to haul a passenger train over the Derby to Manchester route, for, as from 1 July 1968 the route between Matlock and Peak Forest Junction closed completely. The connecting services between Millers Dale and Buxton had ended a year earlier and, as seen here, the south curve onto the Buxton branch had then been disconnected.

Carrying arguably one of the most garish and unsightly headboards ever seen, the LCGB 'Two Cities' railtour of 23 June 1968, from Liverpool Lime Street, traversed no fewer that four separate routes to Manchester during the course of its ambitious itinerary. Seen at Earlestown, awaiting the arrival of 8F No 48033 at the head of the special, is a very presentable Standard 5MT 4-6-0 No 73069.

Chapter 9

Mid-summer steam specials

Just two steam specials operated immediately before the final weekend, both towards the end of July. On 21 July, the Roch Valley Railway Society organised a tour starting at Manchester Victoria and travelling to/from Southport by four different routes. This view shows Lostock Hall's No 45110 en route between Southport and Burscough Bridge on the ex-L&Y route to Wigan Wallgate, shortly before taking the now-lifted spur onto the Preston/Ormskirk line.

Returning from Carnforth and heading for Skipton with the MRTS/SVRS special of 28 July, the train is seen near Bentham, now headed by Standard 4MT 4-6-0s Nos 75019 and 75027 - by this date these being two of the three remaining working members of the class. Notice the burnished brass cab-window frames and No 75027's lined green livery.

Having already run two extremely successful railtours earlier in the year, on 28 July 1968, the Manchester Rail Travel Society, in association with the Severn Valley Railway Society, ran its 'Farewell to BR Steam Tour' from Birmingham New Street. From Stockport to Carnforth via Wigan North Western, motive power was No 70013 Oliver Cromwell. This picture, taken from the remains of the old Boars Head Junction station platform (closed in 1949), shows the extremely unusual ex-LNW signal box that used to control the junction of the former Lancashire Union Joint line to Chorley. The signalbox was closed and demolished when the West Coast Main Line was electrified in the early 1970s.

Having climbed up to Hoghton summit from the Ribble Valley, the distinctive local landmark containing the historic Hoghton Tower provides a dramatic backcloth to Oliver Cromwell approaching Pleasington station on the Preston-Blackburn line with the MRTS/SVRS special of 28 July 1968.

With a reversal in direction at Skipton, the special now takes the section of railway between Skipton and Colne that, although not a target under the Beeching axe and, indeed, a one-time major artery for Yorkshire-Lancashire holiday excursion traffic, closed in January 1970. Seen near Elslack are 'Black Fives' Nos 45073 and 45156.

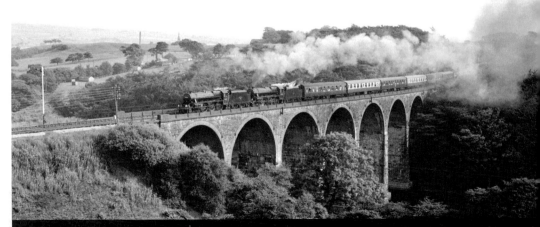

Having travelled via Wigan and Bolton, during their ambitiously circuitous itinerary around Lancashire, Nos 45073 and 45156 head for Blackburn once more, and working hard up-grade, head out across Entwistle Viaduct.

On the final stage of the tour, from Rose Grove to Stockport, and with evening shadows starting to form, the MRTS/SVRS special of 28 July climbs past Cliviger on the Copy Pit route to Todmorden. No 48773 was originally constructed in 1940 by the North British Locomotive Company and, in 1941, was sent to Persia (Iran), becoming Iranian State Railways No 41-109. In 1954, it was no longer required in the Middle East and was sent to the Longmoor Military Railway, as WD No 500. In 1957, it was taken into British Railways (Scottish Region) stock as No 48773 and eventually arrived at Bolton in September 1964. Right at the end of steam, it was transferred to Rose Grove from Bolton in July 1968, before finally being purchased for use on the Severn Valley Railway.

Having taken the now-lifted West Curve at Todmorden, the MRTS/SVRS special heads up the Calder Valley line towards Manchester. The sun now having set well and truly behind the hills, No 48773 is seen on the last few yards before entering Summit Tunnel on the final leg heading towards Stockport.

Chapter 10

1P58 to Blackpool

Memories of 1968

RIGHT A very clean
Lostock Hall 'Black Five'
No 44683 climbs out
of Preston station, with
1P58, the 12:44 Preston
to Blackpool South on
26 December 1967

Until Lostock Hall's 'Black Five' No 45305 worked the last lunchtime 1P58 on 17 May 1968, the 12:44 Preston to Blackpool South (the rear portion of the 09:05 ex-Euston) was the steam passenger train to photograph in the Fylde. As I was working in Kirkham or Lytham at the time, lunches were spent eating sandwiches, waiting with 'Pentax' at the ready! On the days that she was on time, some fine photos were taken; better still if 8P21, the 8F-hauled 10:52 Burnley to Wyre Dock coal train, also came through. And there was always the chance of a local ballast working, but waiting for 3J03, the 13:50 Blackpool North to Manchester parcels, meant being late back!

Then came June, when days were longer, and the other 1P58 was steam. In my younger days, the 17:05 Euston to Blackpool Central was a star performer, a 1B Camden-shedded Royal Scot roaring by the bedroom window in St Anne's - always the fastest train of the day away from Ansdell station. It was years later that I found out the obvious reason - pubs closed at 22:30 and the crew were thirsty!

In 1968 the 17:05 at least ran steam from Preston to Blackpool South; we could ride it and, hopefully, could just photograph it in the light, as departure was at 20:50 (again, hopefully)!

Having used the last bit of sunlight to photograph No 44971 passing Kirkham on 8 June, flash was used on

The study of reporting numbers has always proved to be very involved and a book could easily be written on this subject alone. The problem with referring to a specific train by its reporting number was that the working often shared the same number with more than one train. For main-line expresses, this did not usually apply, as, in most instances there were far fewer trains travelling to one specific destination over the whole route (the down 'Royal Scot' was always 1S57, for example), but local services on secondary and commuter lines were too numerous to each warrant its own numerical description. A single number, therefore, was often allocated to each type of train on each particular route. (Manchester-Blackpool South 'all stations' stoppers all used 2P63, Manchester-Blackpool North stoppers all used 2P64, all Blackburn to Blackpool North stoppers used 2P52 – and so on.) Every day there were two 'portions' of main-line expresses from Euston that, having detached their front sections for these to go forward with their train locos to destinations further north, the remaining parts ran as separate trains to Blackpool South. Being expresses, rather than 'stoppers', they both used the code 1P58. Lostock Hall shed provided the motive power.

the same loco at St Anne's the following Saturday. This last one had been a very poor run, with the engine priming badly, and a max speed of only 38mph before Kirkham, which took all of 19 minutes for 7¾ miles! Not bad for seven coaches!

After riding the narrow-gauge trains at Bressingham the following weekend (Alan Bloom's wife Flora was my parents' bridesmaid way back in 1942) and seeing the Keighley & Worth Valley Railway reopen on 29 June (another milestone event), it was back to '1P58' again, 6 July surprisingly producing a Brush Type 4 on the train. How filthy the diesels were in those days!

The now-preserved No 45305 did the honours on 13 July, clocking 55mph max and 14min to the Kirkham stop, and

58mph at Moss Side, arriving at Lytham in 24½ minutes. My picture that evening was of the train disappearing away from Lytham station, with the signalbox gaslights showing. (1/30th second exposure needed on 50ASA slide film).

And so to 20 July. Driver John Burnett, on an excellent No 45388 plus six coaches, left Preston 15 late and ran well, managing just over 60mph before the Kirkham stop, done in 12min and 68 at Moss Side to arrive in Lytham in 22 minutes. At St Anne's, I even managed to take his photo. However, just think back to that classic steam run made in 1908 on the 17:10 Blackpool Club Train of 11 corridors, 300 tons, when local driver A Traill ran non-stop from Manchester Victoria to Lytham, to arrive eight minutes early on a 60min

schedule! The loco was Aspinall L&Y 7ft 3in 4-4-0 No 1098, rebuilt by George Hughes with superheater, Walschaerts valve-gear and piston valves - just like No 45388.

A very clean No 45388 appeared again in Preston station on 27 July. As this was previously thought to be going to be the last day of steam on the 20:50, someone had put a rosebay willowherb wreath on it. I produced a '1P58' board for the occasion, using a square NE Region type that had been 'exchanged' at Blackpool North shed in 1967 - the LMR ones,

which hung over the smokebox handrail, covered the loco number, so were disliked! It was just possible to photograph No 45388 on its train in Platform 5 (now 3), run under the subway, and join some 70-plus other enthusiasts in the now-packed seven coaches.

I don't know who the crew were, but they did us proud - 72mph at Spen Lane and, after not stopping at Kirkham, running a fast 74 by Moss Side. Between Ansdell and St Anne's, we got up to 55mph… shades of the old 17:05pm! Acceleration away from St Anne's was

ABOVE Lostock Hall driver, John Burnett and his fireman, Mick Halsall look out for the tip from the guard for the 'rightaway' for 1P58 at St Anne's on 20 July 1968

electric; to achieve all of 60mph by Squire's Gate (1½ miles) was tremendous. And we had to stop in Blackpool South platform (another ¾ mile only) and not in the carriage sidings! So, the atmosphere was right for a party!

Normally, No 45388 would have left the coaches in the carriage sidings at Blackpool South, turned and watered, and proceeded back light engine to Preston. Today, however, arrangements were made to stop en-route near my home, a camera flash being fired to let the crew know exactly where.

The fireman then went to the nearby railway telephone to let the signalman at Moss Side know there was a problem with the loco! ...Quite a few of

The Euston train having eventually materialised and the front portion gone forward, No 45388 is seen here slowly picking up speed after a cold start out of Platform 5, heading into the sunset towards the imposing spire of St Walburge's Church.

us enjoyed food and drink that night, at 23:30, including the local Police Constable and Town Councillor. St. Andrews Road South had never seen anything like this! Experimenting with those large PF100 flash bulbs, I even recorded the event on film.

At around midnight, some of us joined the crew for a ride to Preston, getting a lift home in the unlucky one's car. We had made something out of the occasion.

The last week of steam arrived - many of us spending time rushing like headless chickens around the North West. We then learnt that the 20:50 Blackpool and 21.25 Liverpool would be steam on 3 August after all. Thus, after seeing No 75019 make the last two revenue-earning BR freight workings from Heysham to Carnforth in the afternoon, it was time to ride the very last steam to Blackpool. The train, which was packed solid, was hauled by a poorly steaming No 45212 - reported to be due to blocked tubes, this being her last run, and we set no records. The farewell photos were taken on Blackpool South turntable, using the small PF5 expendable flash bulbs - remember them? What a pity Blackpool Tower wasn't lit! In fact it was not until 1998 that I took a photo of a 'Black Five' with the Tower illuminated.

So ended the saga of 1P58. At least No 45212 is preserved, and the reporting number also hangs in my garage. It has actually been out on the main line again… on No 6233. And there are always the photographs and slides to remind us of those now far-off days.

Those 40 years have passed very quickly… I now must get booked on the 1T57 re-run!

BELOW On 27 July 1968, the Barrow portion of the Euston train having been despatched on its way, No 45388 couples onto the rear portion of the train, which, as the Eastern Region reporting number board indicates, will now become 1P58

BELOW On 27 July 1968, the Barrow portion of the Euston train having been despatched on its way, No 45388 couples onto the rear portion of the train, which, as the Eastern Region reporting number board indicates, will now become 1P58

Chapter 11

Last month of steam

And now there are only three

If the reader is seeking fanciful tales or images in any way akin to the glamour and romance of the 'Glorious Years of Steam', then this chapter will almost certainly disappoint. Indeed, for both professional railwaymen and enthusiasts alike, there really was little that was either eminently outstanding or memorable about those agonising last few weeks.

As with any bereavement, it was all merely a particularly painful period that one just had to endure and, in retrospect, I do recall having written elsewhere in the past that one of my greatest wishes in life would have been NOT to have witnessed the end of steam on British Railways. I guess that many more, if faced with a similar fanciful option, would have echoed such sentiments.

But, unlike some who were content to remember happier times and to be able to 'leave it at that', I actually resided within easy walking distance of

RIGHT During a pause in shunting, Lostock Hall driver, Tony 'Yogi Bear' Gillett oils round 'Black Five' No 45407, while standing in Garstang & Catterall Yard with Target 67 on 26 July 1968

THE GRAND FINALE OF BRITISH STEAM

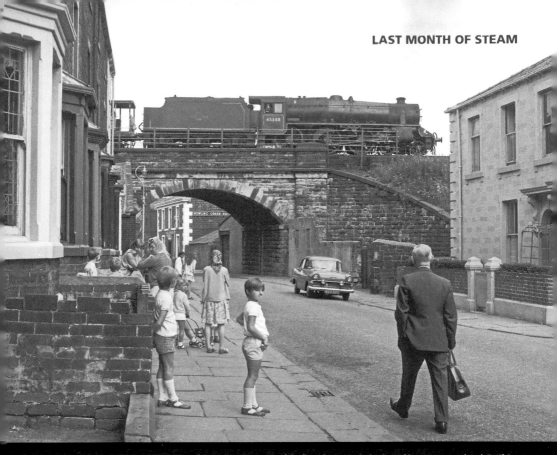

Arch Street, Burnley, 31 July 1968. In the opinion of the author, this is one of the finest 'steam in the landscape' images ever produced. Typifying everything that was synonymous with Lancashire cotton mill country of the 1950s and 1960s, women in slippers and wearing head-squares over hair still in rollers, gossip in this back-street cameo outside their smoke-blackened terraced cottages, while children play on flagstone pathways totally unhindered by parked cars and moving traffic. Apart from the viaduct itself (and perhaps some of the younger observers), everything in this view is no more – indeed even the Bowling Green Hotel has gone. At the rear of the train pictured opposite, with Rose Grove fireman David Hill surveying the scene, No 45388 can be seen slowly banking 8P21 up the hill to Gannow Junction.

BELOW Although much reduced in quantity, steam continued to operate over the Calder Valley line via the Copy Pit route. Here, Rose Grove's 8F No 48410 climbs past Cornholme with a coal working from the Yorkshire coalfields bound for the Lancashire power stations

one of the 'last three' and, I suppose, that gave me little option but to permit myself to be involved to some degree in the poignant death throes. With the assistance of my old pal of very many years, Bob Downham - who had the remarkable foresight to record each detail of every single loco movement that he observed for probably at least ten years before steam ended - let us all now travel back 40 years in time.

In July 1968, the locations of these three final outposts, with the dubious honour thrust upon them of completing the last chapter in the history books, are certainly not celebrity top-ranking names inextricably associated with express passenger locomotives and famous titled trains. Indeed, just about as far from this as it is possible to get, the 'bread-and-butter' duties of Carnforth, Lostock Hall and Rose Grove centre – as they always have done – strictly upon the efficient operation of freight traffic, with the very occasional passenger working thrown-in for good measure. Such moments in the limelight will be brief enough, for even these establishments are officially scheduled to close to steam as from midnight on Sunday 4 August, and, at which time, the curtain will be brought down on steam traction on the British Railways standard gauge.

Yes, currently some of us do seem to be spending most of our weekends engaged in illicit pursuits mainly avoiding the notice of management, while simultaneously attempting to restore a sense of respectability to a fast-disappearing collection of unkempt and rusting relics of a bygone age - still functioning often only on a wing and a prayer, merely because there still are not enough new diesels available to replace them!

Again, yes, we will get the occasional good shot, if the train runs to time and if the sun shines (particularly if it also falls on the single side of the engine that we usually only have had time to clean). Some success is achieved, as the photographs in the following pages will confirm.

However, all of this is merely a drop in the ocean in the general scheme of things… and we know it! The time has come for steam and no-one at all can change decisions that have already been made by that bunch of faceless bureaucrats sitting at desks over 200 miles away in their ivory tower of 222 Marylebone Road.

All we really can do now is to savour the familiar sights, sounds and atmosphere for as long as is possible. The final month proves to be a frenetic one for those privileged to witness the last rites; indeed, it is a mad dash to get to as many locations as possible in order to record as much as one can. That is easier said than done, for few of us can afford our own transport and, on weekdays - when most steam action obviously occurs - there is the added encumbrance of being compelled to go

BELOW On 31 July, No 48340 heads 8P21, the heavily laden 10:50 Burnley Central to Wyre Dock, across Burnley Viaduct. Out of sight in this view is 'Black Five' No 45388, providing banking assistance at the rear as far as Gannow Jct

On 15 June 1968, Rose Grove's No 45350 passes Chaffers Sidings 'box in Nelson with 3J83.

out to work, if only to finance the basic essentials in life - such as adequate film stock for the following weekend's activities. Furthermore, as 'the time' draws ever closer, the ensuing waits at the lineside grow longer and longer – even when one does actually know where to look and at what time of day! Although we try to ignore these, such blatant, facts, steam's life-blood is rapidly ebbing away.

Perhaps the one single positive aspect of this contraction of steam manifests itself in the inevitable coming-together of a large number of individuals from every walk of life and from just about every corner of the country, merely in order to share in such a unique experience. The remarkable fact today, 40 years on, is that the camaraderie that ensued in those final days created lasting friendships that, in the majority of cases, have survived the intervening years. Between us all, we did manage to record a great deal and, for myself, this has nowhere become more apparent than during the course of the researching for this book, where, almost entirely through the offices of my many longstanding friends, I have come to amass well in excess of a thousand photographs - all of which were taken merely in the early 1968 period! Each one of those images is important in its own right, but, clearly, in singling-out a mere fraction to use in the pitifully few pages available here, this feature can but present a mere flavour of what occurred. Notwithstanding that, I sincerely hope the reader will find them sufficiently absorbing without any real necessity to provide lengthy captions and superfluous detail. Images like these speak for themselves and need no tall stories to enhance their impact. This is 1968 as it really was, 'warts and all', and, for me, foolish or fictional embellishments to any such account seem redundant.

By the beginning of July, only five locomotive types remain in service; the bulk of these being the ubiquitous Stanier Class 5MT 4-6-0s and Class 8F 2-8-0s, along with five Standard 4MT 4-6-0s and a solitary example each of the Standard 5MT 4-6-0s and Britannia Pacifics. All, bar one, of the regular steam passenger workings have disappeared and, apart from a tiny handful of parcels trains, all steam action is (at least, on paper), supposedly restricted to freight and station pilot duties and the, by now, inevitably quite frequent enthusiasts' specials.

According to official loco diagrams, the final regular steam-hauled passenger is supposed to be the 1P58 (Saturdays Only) 20:50 Preston to Blackpool South (a portion of a through train from London Euston) rostered for a Lostock Hall Stanier 5MT.

After completion of its duties in stabling the stock, the loco is then booked to return light from Blackpool to Preston, to officiate as station pilot – or, more specifically, to provide steam heat for the two sleeping cars that it will attach (along with a BG) to the rear of the 20:30 Windermere-London at around 22:30. Although little-recognised as such, technically, this too, is a 'passenger' working, albeit merely for a matter of a few hundred yards and only between the platforms at Preston. It is not the only example, either. A similar task involves another 10D loco, in the removal at 03:46 of two more sleeping cars plus a BG from 1P54, the 23:15 Euston-Windermere. The BG later going forward at 04:10 attached to a Manchester-Blackpool parcels, these vehicles are stabled in a bay platform with the loco steam-heating them until around 08:00.

LAST MONTH OF STEAM

Despite the official edict, for a variety of reasons, other steam passenger workings still do occur, even if somewhat sporadically and, at times, not even to the knowledge of the 'grapevine', until after it is all over.

On parcels traffic, there are now only four regular turns. The first is an 'out-and-home' working, booked for a Lostock Hall 'Black Five', namely 3P00, the 02:50 Preston to Colne and 3P20 19:14 (MX) Colne to Preston. On the main line, there is 3P24, the (MSO) Preston to Barrow (also a Lostock Hall 'Black Five') and 1P92, the 20:28 Barrow to Preston (a Carnforth 'Black Five').

On the freight side, workings are equally elusive and, working timetables for these appear to have been published more as a 'guide' than for any other ulterior motive.

In the Preston area on weekdays, about 20 or so steam freights still pass by (but not all necessarily through Preston station itself). These include local trip workings between the various yards in the area with those at Garstang, Horwich, Chorley, Deepdale and Courtaulds – the latter two being on the truncated former Longridge branch. Ballast trains also run, as required, between the Preston and Lancaster areas, and longer-distance general-merchandise traffic traverses the various routes between Carnforth, Warrington (Arpley), Bolton (Burnden Jct), Manchester (Ancoats) and Liverpool Edge Hill. Block-train oil-tanker traffic also runs on three days a week between Heysham and Darwen.

However, by far the majority of the remainder of the traffic consists of coal trains between the Bickershaw and Parkside Collieries (in the Wigan area) and Whitebirk Power Station (just beyond Blackburn), this complemented by additional workings between Rose Grove or Burnley Central and Wyre Dock or Burn Naze (Fleetwood). There are also two or three workings over the Copy Pit route, usually as far as Healey Mills Yard, near Wakefield in Yorkshire.

Most of the routes that this freight traffic uses pass through rugged and hilly terrain in or at the edge of the Pennines. Consequently, several are heavily graded in places and feature impressive engineering works. The Bolton-Blackburn line, for instance, provides hard work for trains in both directions towards a summit near Sough

Tunnel, but particularly so northbound on the gradients of at mainly 1-in-73 for the first six miles out of Bolton. In these final days, the actual tracking-down of steam workings during daylight hours on the route is far more problematical!

On the line over into Yorkshire via Copy Pit, there are similar gradients for five miles from Gannow Jct to Copy Pit Summit and, in the opposite direction, the route is even steeper, with westbound trains being faced with almost four miles of 1-in-65 on a very winding set of tracks all the way up from Stansfield Hall Jct, Todmorden. In order to provide the rear-end assistance that most trains need, there are usually at least two 8F banking engines regularly out-stationed from Rose Grove at Todmorden. Additional bonuses for the photographer in East Lancashire are the eye-catching urban viaducts providing such significant landmarks both in Burnley and also in Accrington, where they tower over much of the surrounding townscapes.

Situated close to the gateway to the Lake District and the Cumberland Coast ('Cumbria' is a word that will not be coined for another six years!), the remaining steam turns from Carnforth

GOODS TRAINS
MUST STOP HERE
TO PIN DOWN BRAKES

The very last steam-worked 7P80, the 14:35 Wyre Dock to Burnley Central coal empties, passes Weeton signalbox on 2 August 1968.

shed continue to penetrate deep into similarly highly scenic regions. With the Lakeland mountains rising sharply from the coastal plain on the right and breathtaking sea-views to the left, a small handful of workings pass over two spectacular estuary viaducts and, for those workings continuing onwards to Barrow, there are also ascents in each direction of the notorious Lindal Bank.

Away from the coast, steam still visits various other goods yards on a daily basis; these including Kendal and Windermere. Yet other occasional workings penetrate into the Dales as far

as Giggleswick and even to Skipton.

We shall concentrate our review on the calendar month between 4 July and 4 August 1968 and commence this by looking at a day of the week when steam activity might normally be considered to be at its peak. A national 'work-to-rule' has, however, been in place for several days now and the detrimental effect of this upon operations is becoming increasingly apparent. The country's rail network had already been thrown into disarray from 24 June by this dispute of the NUR, before ASLEF then joined in the affray soon afterwards. The situation is to endure for 12 days, with chaos worsening, particularly when the quite incredulous fact is considered that, at this period in the 1960s, more than 20 per cent of day-to-day railway work is currently being conducted during 'overtime'.

These final weeks for steam have, equally unfortunately, also coincided with the annual holidays (or 'Wakes Weeks') in several East Lancashire towns, with the knock-on effect from further (planned) cancellations to other freight workings. Most noticeable will be the absence of the otherwise quite frequent Parkside and Bickershaw to Whitebirk coal workings – which, traditionally, provide much of Rose Grove's work.

Nevertheless, some trains do appear to have been unaffected. During the small hours of this Thursday morning, at Preston station, the Euston sleepers have arrived on time at 03:46 and 'Black Five' No 45110 is there waiting to remove them from the main train (which will now proceed northwards behind its usual diesel) and to place them first into Platform 3 and then into Platform 5 Bay, remaining coupled-up until 08:00 to keep any occupants warm in their bunks.

Further north, at Carnforth, the sole-surviving Standard 5MT No 73069 (10A) – a recent transfer from Bolton – also soon sets out at 06:30 with 'No 50 Target', for a planned itinerary largely centred upon shunting the extensive sidings in the Heysham Harbour area. Within minutes of this departure, the yard is also to see 'No 48 Target' depart for Ulverston behind No 44758 (10A), followed by 6P45, the 06:25 Carnforth-Barrow, with No 75048 (10A) - one of the five surviving (but not all necessarily active) Standard 4MT 4-6-0s. After a short lull, it is soon the turn of No 44963 (10A) to set out on Target 61, with four loaded ballast wagons, heading for Sandside (on the former branch to Hincaster Jct) and then onwards to Grange-over-Sands. Finally, 'Target 46' sets out at 12:35, with No 45134 (10A) and loaded domestic coal wagons, on the Kendal tripper. No sooner has this departed than No 44758 returns to base at around 12:45 with 8P76, the 09:30 Barrow-Carnforth, conveying 12 empty soda-ash wagons, which it now proceeds to deposit in the yards to await onwards despatch to the Northwich area.

Over at Heysham Harbour, Lostock Hall's No 45318 is shunting alongside

LAST MONTH OF STEAM

RIGHT A Royal Mail train that also continued with steam right until the very end. 1P92, the 20:28 Barrow to Huddersfield parcels was regularly hauled by a Carnforth 'Black Five' as far as Preston. Here, on 2 August, at a platform bestrewn with mailbags, 'BRUTE' trolleys and miscellaneous barrows, No 44781 has just arrived with 1P92's final steam working and is preparing to come off the train

No 73069 in the yards, having arrived on 7P11, the 10:50 Preston Ribble Sidings-Heysham and delivering no fewer than 52 loaded wagons, the contents of most of which are undoubtedly destined for Ulster. Having completed this task, No 45318 prepares to depart again with 6P52, the 14:30 to Preston NU. Also patiently waiting close by is No 44874 (10A), ready to follow 6P52 down the main line to Preston with 5F24, the 15:05 to Warrington Arpley, conveying another load of general merchandise from across the water. It being a perfect example of the numerous uneconomic workings that recent removals of steam servicing facilities at destinations around the ever-contracting periphery of steam operation has created, No 44874 will return later that evening light-engine all the way back to Carnforth shed. To round-off this, our first day of observations, the 18:40 (TThO) Darwen-Heysham oil tankers is running and this arrives at its destination on time at around 21:00 behind No 44735 (10A), which has run-round its train at Morecambe.

The following morning, having observed both No 44709 (10A) passing through Preston somewhat late, at 07:45, with 5F16, the 04:15 Carnforth-Edge Hill and then No 45269 (10D) running back to shed from the station at 08:15 following its sleeping-car steam-heat duty, we head off towards East Lancashire in order to witness operations based on the steam hub of Rose Grove.

En route, at Wilpshire, No 45096 (10F) is seen topping the bank at 08:50, unusually running very early with 'Target 19', the 09:12 Blackburn (Darwen St) to Clitheroe trip working, with which it will return to Blackburn shortly before 14:00 after some hours of shunting. In sidings at Blackburn's Whitebirk Power Station, sits

No 48247 (10F), which has arrived at 10:16 on Rose Grove's Target 83. After shunting until noon, the 8F will return with a load of empty wagons to Rose Grove. Meanwhile, over at Padiham Power Station (situated at the stub-end of the erstwhile Great Harwood Loop which is now only connected at the Rose Grove end), No 48666 (10F) has arrived at 10:30 with 'Target 86', which is another local duty, this one tripping as required between Burnley Central Yard and both Padiham and Huncoat power stations.

Moving onwards to Rose Grove itself, a longer-distance working soon appears shortly after our arrival. Struggling on the steep gradient up from Burnley Central, No 48400 (10F) passes Gannow Jct on time, with 8P21, the 10:50 Burnley Central-Wyre Dock coal train. Given the weight of this visibly well-loaded working, its pace appears unusually brisk until the reason for this soon makes itself apparent. Bystanders in the street stop to watch as the huge train thrashes its way off the lofty viaduct up the hill towards Barracks Station with No 45394 (10A) noisily assisting from the rear. The two loco-

the 02:50 Preston-Colne parcels – a turn otherwise consistently worked by Lostock Hall. There is another aspect of No 45394 that is noticed to be unusual; it is probably now the only remaining locomotive still bearing the distinctive larger 'Scottish Region-type' cab-side numerals and full lining-out, all clearly resulting from a visit to St Rollox Works some years earlier.

The inevitable repercussions of the 'work-to-rule' are evident and the consequent lull of just under an hour is eventually, but noisily, brought

motives soon disappearing from view, their audible progress continues to be heard for many more minutes until the banker eases off in the vicinity of Rose Grove station in order to retire to the shed. This process is a regular duty, but it is unusual to see a Carnforth engine involved, especially as this 'Black Five' has arrived in the area today on 3P00,

to an conclusion with the arrival of No 48062 (10F) thrashing over the junction off the Padiham line with 'Target 92' to draw its load of power station empties into the 'Down Grid' sidings. Some minutes afterwards, No 48247 (10F) also struggles into the yard, returning with yet another load of empties from Whitebirk. With a further load of coal now behind the tender, it is not long before the insatiable No 48062 sets off for another trip down to Padiham.

It is, indeed, a busy day for Padiham, but this is not untypical. Targets 86 & 83 have arrived separately in the 'Up Grid' sidings and No 48666 (10F) and No 48247 (10F) now combine forces to work forward down the branch with yet more coal. At 13:53, and running a 1/2 hour late, No 48348 (10F) also draws out of the 'Up Grid' with 6P32, the 13:10 coal to Wyre Dock. Ten minutes later, No 48340 (10F) follows it out onto the main line with 8P32, the 13:40 Rose Grove-Ribble Sidings.

Another lull in traffic occurs, so there is time for a shed visit, during which No 44899 (10F) arrives light from the Preston direction at around 16:00, having previously worked a special ballast train to an unidentified destination. Exactly another hour later, No 48348, which has evidently disposed of its train at Wyre Dock in extra-rapid time and, there being no further work for it, also arrives back on shed light-engine at around 17:00. Not far behind No 48348, follows No 48400 (10F) with 7P80, the 14:35 Wyre Dock-Burney Central coal empties.

For No 48666 there is now a chance

to round off its day of mundane Padiham trip workings with a longer-distance foray at the head of 5J10, the 19:05 Burnley Central-Moston general merchandise.

The yellow-stripe celebrity 8F No 48773 has, this evening, been earmarked for a special carriage-shunting duty and is being prepared for this. Leaving shed at about 18:00, it sets out for Colne. At this period in time, a supply of passenger stock is still stored in the carriage shed at Colne and, it being the start of that town's 'Wakes Week', there are several additional trains leaving Colne this evening for various holiday destinations. To augment the available resources (which won't amount to very much in 1968) an 11-coach ECS special, powered by No 48247 (10F), arrived last night from the Manchester direction to provide the balance of the necessary requirements. Sorting all of this into the required formations will take a while, but the task no sooner completed, the engine is back on shed by 22:00 – allowing the crew a final pint before closing time!

Five special trains are booked to depart from Colne between 19:30 and 23:55; two of these - to Heysham and to Liverpool – will consist of four-car

LEFT Stanier 8F No 48340, a former Northwich engine until that shed closed, passes Poulton-le-Fylde No 5 cabin, with 8P19, the 12:00 Burnley Central-Burn Naze coal train. The tracks to the right, known as Poulton curve, are those of the direct line from Fleetwood to Blackpool North, over which there was a passenger service until the 1960s

LAST MONTH OF STEAM

DMUs and two more - to Paignton and to Euston – will be diesel-hauled. Rose Grove shed, however, has the honour of providing No 45156 (formerly Ayrshire Yeomanry) as motive power for 1T55, the 19:30 Colne to Newquay. Admittedly the train is only to be three coaches in length, but for those 'in the know', this will provide the unique chance to travel behind steam, as far as Stockport, up the notorious Baxenden Bank with its first two miles at about 1-in-40 from Accrington – a very rare opportunity with steam by this time. (At Stockport, the train will combine with a main portion that has most likely started its own journey at Manchester Piccadilly.)

Leaving all of these operations to continue in our absence, we move over to the Preston area now, just in time to witness an hour or so of relatively intense activity. At shortly before 19:00, the wheel flanges of its load of bogie oil tankers squealing around the sharp curves, No 48393 (10F) slowly passes through Preston's East Lancs line platforms with 4P20, the 18:12 (FO) Heysham Moss-Darwen and at 19:02 No 48765 (10D) climbs Farington Curve with 7N61, the 18:20 Farington Jct to Healey Mills, which,

due to the dispute, very unusually has today started from Preston NU yard and which will be terminated at Rose Grove as no guard is available tonight beyond that point. Equally curiously, No 45394 (10A) arrives light at Lostock Hall shed from Rose Grove. It will be recalled that we had observed it earlier in the day on the 10D diagram which should have brought it back to Preston on the 3P20 19:14 Colne-Preston parcels. Its place on that duty has tonight been taken by a Type 2 diesel – which is also very unusual. Why this should have occurred is unclear, as No 45394 is to remain based at 10D for another week, being used on local trip workings and even back on 3P00/3P20 the following Monday!

On the main line south of Preston, clearly having spent some time remarshalling in Ribble Sidings Yard, No 45200 (10A) is seen at 20:02, pulling slowly out of the Up Through onto the Up Slow at Skew Bridge 'box, with 5F24, the 15:05 Heysham to Warrington Arpley. As soon as the points are set back, No 44806 (10D) arrives from the opposite direction on the down slow, running light from Lostock Hall shed to Preston station, in order to take up its allotted nocturnal task as station pilot.

Meanwhile, No 45200 on 5F24 gets no further than Farington Jct, where it arrives at 20:10 and proceeds to sit here on the main line until 20:59. Having allowed some 12 trains to pass by, it now sets its train backwards over the fast lines into the up yard. It remains here until 21:46, when, quite amazingly, No 45394 shows up again to exchange places with No 45200; the latter immediately disappearing onto shed, by now probably short on coal and water. 5F24 eventually sets off again, some 5½ hours after its booked time.

Saturday, 6 July, and although the 'work-to-rule' has at long last been settled, it is too late to alter the workings and rosters, so many trains are still not running. Local trips, however, appear to have escaped relatively unscathed and we start our day back at Farington Jct at 06:35 to discover No 45444 (10D) already hard at work in the yard preparing its load for 'Target 63', the Deepdale and Courtaulds turn up the old Longridge branch.

At shortly before 07:00, the Down Fast signals are pulled off and No 44877 (10A) soon appears, running at speed light-engine back to its home shed. All the depots in the Liverpool area having

LAST MONTH OF STEAM

Back in Kendal yard, the cleaning is completed and more shunting takes place

already been closed to steam for two months by this time, 5F16, the 04:15 Carnforth- Edge Hill, is one of those examples of 'unbalanced workings' where steam still works into areas from which it is otherwise banned. If this had been a weekday, part of the diagram would usually have included 5P23, the 11:45 (SX) Ribble Sidings-Carnforth.

As an indication of the confusion that knock-on effects of the 'work-to-rule' are still creating, at 09:25 our old friend No 45394 is still making valiant attempts to get back to its rightful home, now coming off shed running

light to Preston station ready to work the 09:58 (SO) Preston-Barrow parcels.

Inter-departmental communications are clearly in a flux, for that train had already been cancelled by Control, causing No 45394 later to return back to 10D. It may be of interest to note that, of the 19 reliefs, specials and ECS workings scheduled to pass through Preston today, nearly half appear to have been cancelled. Indeed, the one regular steam passenger turn of the week, the 20:50 to Blackpool South, is worked by D1618, as 1P79, the main portion of the train to Windermere, is another casualty of the

THE GRAND FINALE OF BRITISH STEAM

dispute and the remaining Blackpool portion is worked by the rostered 1P79 loco. The sleeping car heating duty also having been cancelled, the only other steam working to be observed is No 45025 (10A) on 4P21, the 13:35 Darwen-Heysham Moss oil tankers and even that only gets on its way a full hour after its booked time.

By the following week, matters are slowly beginning to return to normal and, after a reasonably quiet day steam-wise, on the Monday nearly all booked diagrams are back in business.

Wednesday, 10 July could be considered a typical day, for both steam and photography. With torrential downpours lashing many parts of the country, the sun manages to shine through in the North West and the following regular workings are observed in the Preston area. In order of appearance (use the reporting numbers to refer to the previous tables for train details): 3P00-45073 (10D), steam-heating sleeping cars off previous night's 1P54 and then shunting ballast wagons in Dock St Sidings-44806 (10D), Target 66-45394 (10A), 5P02-44781 (10A), 7P11-44971 (10D), 6P52-45407 (10D), 8P21-48062 (10F), 5P23-45025 (10A), 10-coach ECS to Pitt St Sidings (north of station) arriving at 12:40-45200 (10A), Target 78-45318 (10D), Target 63-45110 (10D), 8P19-48340 (10F), conveying track-laying unit to NU Yard-75019 (10A), 6P32-48493 (10F), 6P52-44971 (10D), 5F24-44874 (10A), 6P16-45305 (10D), Target 70-45055 (10D), another 10-coach ECS - off the East Lancs line arriving at 19:30-45200 (10A), 7N99-48493 (10F), steam-heating sleeping cars off 1P54-44806 (10D), 3P20-45073 (10D) and finally 1P92-44897 (10A). No 48340 (10F), as noted above, arriving at Blackpool North shed off 8P19 is soon appropriated to work a special Blackpool North to Morecambe train of empty stock and it will return to Preston even later on with more empty stock which, curiously, must have come from Morecambe.

On Friday, 12 July, observations in the Rose Grove area reveal a similar typical pattern of work: 7N78-48666 (10F), 8P21-48773 (10F), westbound special coal empties from Burnley Central (probably to Parkside or Bickershaw)-45073 (10D), unidentified westbound coal-48400 (10F), Target 86-48393 (10F), Target 92-48730 (10F), 7N78-48666 (10F), 8P19-48062 (10F),

RIGHT A diesel
working during
previous weeks,
with Morecambe
Bay as a backcloth,
on 27 July 1968, No
45025 unexpectedly
materialises with
3P24, the 09:58 (SO)
Preston to Barrow
parcels andis
observed skirting
the coastline near
Kents Bank

Target 86-48393 (10F), light to 10D then to work 6P16-75027 (10A), 6P32-48493 (10D), 7P65-44781 (10A), 8P32-43893 (10F), 8P20-48765 (10D) and 7P80-48773 (10F).

Among the 20 additional or altered trains for the Preston and Accrington town holidays are two on 19 July which are steam powered, the 1T55 22:20 Preston-Manchester Victoria, which forms part of the 23:34 Manchester Victoria-Paignton, being powered by No 44781 (10A), with the engine penetrating an area nominally banned to steam, since it has started out from Blackpool North at 21:20 with its empty stock and regular steam also no longer travels through to Manchester. Meanwhile, likewise 1H11, the 23:35 Accrington-Stockport works through to Stockport, this time via Bolton, with No 45156 (10F) to attach its five coaches to the 01:10 Manchester Piccadilly-Euston. Obviously, these essentially nocturnal operations provide little in the way of opportunity for photography, but certainly No 45156 produces much in the way of fireworks for those interested in loco performance, particularly on the climb up to Sough Tunnel over the Blackburn to Bolton line, achieving 65mph downhill to Bolton.

The latter route is, of course, one of the most scenic of those still available to steam in 1968 but, with the recent closing of the Manchester Division sheds, daytime workings have now become extremely scarce. It is because of this that a favourite (if not the only) subject for photography for some time previously has been the 13:35 (SO) Colne to Manchester Red Bank empty parcels train. This became a Rose Grove turn after the closure of Newton Heath and can now turn up with just about any class of motive power at its head. In July, however, it will see steam haulage on the 13th only, when No 44781 (10A) appears.

Over at Carnforth on 15 July, Britannia No 70013 Oliver Cromwell has departed in steam to Crewe for boiler attention and, while in Works, it is planned for the paintwork to be touched up and re-varnished in preparation for the final railtour duties, which it will resume on 21 July. On 18 July, an unusual sight hereabouts is No 44874 (10A) working a ten-coach 13:55 Barrow - Morecambe relief. Another working out of Barrow during the evening of 23 July, presumably replacement for a failed DMU, saw No 45017 heading three Mk1 coaches towards Carnforth, this in fact constituting the last steam-hauled passenger train on the Furness line.

The main part of the 'Belfast Boat Express' diagram having gone diesel at the beginning of May, the short leg as far as Morecambe with the Sunday morning 06:55 departure from Heysham occasionally still saw steam haulage, an old boat train favourite, No 45342 for example, finding use on 21 July.

Although, previously on 22 June, No 44758 (10A) had been seen in Harrison's Sidings, north of Shap, at 11:00 ready to leave for the south with loaded hopperwagons, that was thought to have been the last time that a steam-working of any type behind a BR loco in regular service occurred so far north. Nevertheless, on 20 July, No 45017 (10A) reaches Tebay from Carnforth with ballast and two further steam engines are believed to have also got this far on 27 July, although no details are to hand for these, the last steam workings through the Lune Gorge.

At this, the very end of steam at Carnforth, the policy with regard to laying-off engines is to not coal them after they return from their penultimate trip, regardless of where the final turn might go to, and the instruction is that the remaining contents of the tender

ABOVE An absolutely
spotless Carnforth
'Black Five' No 45390
heads out of Barrow
with 8P76, the 08:55
Barrow to Carnforth,
on 2 August 1968. This
is almost certainly the
final eastbound freight
working from Barrow

the turntable and water column were removed from Windermere station yard on Saturday 27 July. It is a fact that they have seen little use in recent times, as the Carnforth engine on the daily trip working, 'Target 47', works down the branch tender-first and only takes water in Kendal goods yard when necessary. No 45134 (10A) is on this duty on 22 July, 45025 (10A) on 23 July, 44735 (10A) on 24/25 July and 44894 (10A) on 31 July/1 August.

are to be used up on the last working. This potentially dangerous edict does not appear to have been issued at either 10D or 10F! Nevertheless, on 26 July, No 45394 (10A) works the 13:05 (SX) Carnforth-Skipton freight, being noted with the words 'not to be coaled' chalked on its tender, its final trip being made on Target 46, the 12:35 (SX) Carnforth-Kendal and 18:20 return on the following day, duties which it later appears to have accomplished without embarrassment.

All passenger workings down the Windermere branch having been made diesel duties some time previously,

This is not the end of the story of steam to Windermere, however. Even during this, the final countdown, there are a number of footplatemen who will always prefer working with steam. To them, the realisation that they are within days of a momentous change that is going to affect their lives, it goes without saying that one or two will actively seek opportunities to have a 'last final fling'. On Monday 29 July, Driver Peter Norris books on duty at Lostock Hall in order to collect the loco rostered to work 2P83, the 08:15 Preston to Windermere passenger and its balanced return at the head of 1P27, the 11:00 Windermere-Crewe. Somehow, the rostered Brush Type 4, D1855, has mysteriously managed to 'fail' on shed – although the reasons surrounding this remain unclear - and the other three or four Class 25s close by, allegedly, already all have booked duties. Some fairly reliable sources suggest that a certain 'steam enthusiast' employed in Preston Control just possibly might have been involved in more than an element of collusion in permitting 'Black Five' No 45110 to be prepared for the job. Indeed, there are also suggestions circulating that it is now intended to use steam on the duty for the whole of the remaining week. Sadly, for reasons about to be revealed, the latter consideration just will not occur.

All goes well, No 45110 is in good mechanical order and the five-coach train runs to time throughout its northbound journey. However, things do start to go awry immediately upon arrival at the Windermere terminus. Today, forty years on, Driver Norris openly acknowledges that he had obviously not read any of the Notices at shed properly and that his enthusiasm had paved the way to become unstuck, facing him with an uncomfortable dilemma. Upon looking for the turntable in order to turn his engine, Pete is horrified to discover that there is just a gaping hole in the ground where this really ought to have been. Not only that, but the water column has also disappeared from its own familiar location! Both items have been removed for scrap a mere two days previously!

A tender-first return, although unsatisfactory, is not impossible – indeed, it is the only real option. An abortive attempt is made to replenish the tender during the stopover from a hosepipe linked to the station toilet water tap, but clearly this is going to take too long and departure time is fast approaching. There is believed still to be a working column in the goods yard at Kendal, but this will not solve the problem of turning the loco. Pete's choice now is either to run to Carnforth MPD to turn and run back light engine, but thereby delay his return train (which would require some explaining to the powers-that-be!), or he can take a chance and run tender-first! Although, by this date, much of the trip work for the remaining 'Black Fives' does involve an element of tender-first running at slow speed, the major issue here is that No 45110's return job is at the head of a Class 1 express passenger and, not only that, but with a first booked stop not scheduled until Lancaster! So, 1P27 sets out regardless for Preston, but, with little water remaining in the tender, there is no alternative but to halt at the column on the platform-end at Carnforth. In order then to make up time, some exhilarating running ensues, especially on the straight, fast stretches between Lancaster and Preston (some say 74mph is reached!) and with only a minimal delay… all things considered!

Clearly, these matters never seem to be isolated ones and, come the following day, steam returns yet again to passenger work on the branch! This time, however, no-one has planned what does occur. Shortly after leaving Windermere, the 09:00 DMU to Morecambe fails with a burnt-out starter motor. The 'Thunderbird' that eventually arrives to the rescue is 'Black Five' No 44894 (10A), which, more than likely, is 'Target 47' loco today and probably already in the Kendal area anyway.

During this, the final week for steam, an excess of empty wagons at Whitebirk Power Station is probably the cause of the first appearance of the Whitebirk-Bickershaw train for a while, with

No 48665 (10F) being used on 27/29 July and No 48340 (10F) on 30 July. Most minerals turns are to Padiham power station, and on the Preston line, where the daytime trains are 8P21/7P80, 6P32/7P33/7N99, 7N87/7N68. No 48493 is on 7N87 on 30 July. On 31 July, No 48340 (10F) is on 8P21, (banked by No 45388 (10D) from Burnley Central to Gannow Jct), No 48665 (10F) on 6P32 and No 48393 (10F) on a special Class 8 Burnley Central to Burn Naze, returning on 7N68. Apart from the two workings described above, steam over the Copy Pit route into Yorkshire is scarce.

On Thursday 1 August, fireman John Fletcher and his driver Cliff Nelson book-on at Lostock Hall ready to collect the engine booked to work 7P11, the 10:50 Ribble Sidings-Heysham – a regular 10D duty and with No 45407 chalked-up on the roster-board for them. They are told to wear clean overalls, as 'somebody from the press' will be accompanying them. Eventually it transpires that this 'somebody' is to be a junior reporter from the Sunday

On 9 July, 'Target 48' is seen with a slightly less clean No 75048, returning to Carnforth along the sea wall at Grange-over-Sands. Notice the camping coaches stabled in the sidings opposite the signalbox.

Times who, they are told, is writing a feature on the end of steam. What they are not prepared for, however, is that the reporter turns out to be an attractive young woman clad in a particularly short mini-skirt! What John recalls most vividly of that day (apart from the mini-skirt, that is) is the fact that the journey is to be extensively delayed, due to a tanker train having derailed itself in Morecambe, causing No 45407 to spend a considerable time 'inside' at Oubeck Loop – in the middle of nowhere! For the record, we do have the name of that cub-reporter – one Anne Robinson!

John today wonders what her 'Points of View' may have been about this particular assignment!

In spite of being the second week of Preston Town Holidays, steam engines are very active on local shunts in the Preston area during the first two days of August. On 1 Aug, 'Target 63' has 48775 (10D), Target 66-48723 (10D), Target 67-45260 (10D), Target 70-44806 (10D) and Target 78-45212 (10D); 45110 (10D) has worked 3P00/3P20. The last remaining Ivatt 4MT 2-6-0 No 43106 is also steamed on this date and at 14:00 leaves the shed for the last time,

ABOVE On 2 August 1968, No 75048, at the head of the very last steam-worked trip working from Ulverston, passes over Arnside Viaduct, proceeding on its way entirely un-noticed by daytrippers sunbathing on the beach. They would, perhaps, not act in quite the same way had 'Target 48' passed by 40 years in the future!

heading initially towards Bescot and then towards a new life on the Severn Valley Railway.

At Rose Grove, No 45287 (10F) is provided to work 3T41, a 15-coach special empty stock working from East Lancs to Blackpool North, passing Preston at 11:15 before then retiring light to Lostock Hall shed. Nos 48400 and 48493 are on Rose Grove to Padiham coal trip workings.

No 48519 is on Copy Pit banking duties. No 48665 runs light engine from Rose Grove to Ribble Sidings to head 5P23. Sister engine No 48666 has already been cleaned up on Rose Grove shed in preparation for the depot's very last passenger working – one of the 4 August specials. Meanwhile, it has

headed 6P31, the 04:05 Rose Grove-Wyre Dock, before running light back to shed. No 48727 (10F) works 6P32 and the regular follow-on turns, 7P33 and 7N99, as far as Rose Grove. No 48730 has an equally hectic day, working 8P21, then 7P80 as far as Lostock Hall, where it is replaced by another loco, to permit it to visit Lostock Hall shed before returning to Ribble Sidings to work 7N68 as far as Rose Grove. On this date, No 48773 has arrived on shed at 02:45 from Healey Mills, and then works its final freight turn of all at the head of 5J10 to Moston.

Friday 2 August is the last day of full-scale steam freight working anywhere. At Carnforth, No 45025 (10A) is travelling about the region on the inspection saloon. No 44709 departs from Windermere with the very last steam departure of all with the princely sum of two empty coal wagons in tow. On both 8P76, the 08:55 Barrow-Carnforth and the 13:05 to Skipton, these have 45390 (10A), Target 46-48665 (10A), Target 47-44709 (10A), Target 48-75048 (10A), Target 49-75019 (10A), Target 61-45231 (10A), 5F24-48493 (10F). On 1P92, the final steam working on all of the Barrow-Huddersfield parcels, No 44781 (10A), with Carnforth's legendary Ted Fothergill at the helm, admittedly with a light weight load, is reputed to have touched around 90mph at one point on its dash to Preston.

In the Preston area, we have 3P00/3P20-45407 (10D), Target 70-45318 (10D), 'Target 78'-45212 (10D), 7P11, returning light to 10D-45287 (10F). The last steam freight out of the Fylde is 7P33-48423 (10F), which then goes on to work 7N99, and the last one into the Fylde is 8P20-48727 (10F), which returns light. The 21:25 Preston-Liverpool, by now normally a diesel turn, is to see steam again twice during this final week and tonight, No 45260 (10D) does the honours.

Rose Grove locos are equally active

today, on the following duties: Target 19-45156, 05:20 Preston NU-Healey Mills-48723 (10F), 8P21/7P80-48278 (10F), 5J10-probably 48167 (10F) (no front number plate), 8F43-48400 (10F) returning engine and brake van to Rose Grove, 6P32/7P33/7N99-48423 (10F), 5F24-48493 (10F), 8P20/7N68-48727 (10F). No 48519 (10F) is also noted on a westbound freight and No 48393 (10F) arrives even later on a ballast. No 48666 is on Copy Pit banking duties and, upon returning from Todmorden, it enters the depot yard and promptly derails itself on the extremely dubious trackwork hereabouts, thus causing a major obstruction until it is put back onto the rails. Mobile once more, it is not worth the time and trouble to repair any damage sustained, and is promptly banished to a siding – its place on the special now being allocated to No 48773, which is coincidentally stood close by. Although No 48666 does not appear to need much work to put it right, it joins the end of a line of other withdrawn locomotives which already consist of: 44690/899/5096/350/82/97/447, 4806 2/115/247/57/323/84/410/48/51. The following are observed in steam here today: 45156,48167/91/340/8/93/423/

LAST MONTH OF STEAM

RIGHT With only days
to go before closure,
Rose Grove shed had
resembled more an
'Open Day' atmosphere
than a working steam
shed, with scores -
perhaps even a few
hundred - enthusiasts,
photographers and
'locals' wandering
around the yard. Here,
infants from a nearby
children's crèche have
their first (and last)
glimpses of steam
locomotives

519/666/ 715/27/30/73 (all 10F) also 45407 (10D).

Saturday 3 August is a much quieter day, Carnforth depot appearing to provide most of the action. The first movement off shed is with No 45342 (10A) on 6P42, followed 2½ hours later by the early-running Target 47 with No 44709. Upon arrival at Kendal, driver Watson Sowerby (formerly of Kirkby Stephen depot) watches on in amazement as his steed is groomed in the goods yard for its final departure. It is now the turn of No 45134 (10A) to make a trip to Lancaster Castle Yard, where it will shunt until 11:00 before returning with a brake van to 10A. No 45231 (10A) works a Class 9 special ballast from Waterslack Quarry to Farington Jct (arriving at 11:54) then, after taking coal and water, runs light back from Lostock Hall shed to Carnforth at 12:22, via Farington Curve. This working may well have been an extension to Canforth's (SO) Target 61.

On the (SO) itinerary for 'Target 49', No 75019 is observed mid-morning on the first of a couple of Carnforth-Heysham trip workings that it will undertake today. The very last working

member of its class, it is later observed passing through Hest Bank tender-first at 16:00 with a heavy train of vans from Heysham, on what is believed to be the last steam-worked freight train on BR. Of the other class members so very recently active, No 75027, with its chimney sacked, has joined the preserved locomotives lined up near the turntable and No 75048 has gravitated to the dump at the north end of the yard. Apart from the workings itemised above, only two other engines are observed to be in steam on shed today – these being Nos 45025 and 45390; Indeed, most of the other working Class Fives have gone to Lostock Hall for the following day's railtours and few will ever return.

Over in East Lancashire, but a single special freight is observed. No 48715 (10F) has been provided for an additional Rose Grove to Ribble Sidings turn (which passes Lostock Hall at 12:29), the loco then runs light to Moss Lane Jct to reverse direction, permitting it to return to Rose Grove shed chimney-first. In the absence of any other observations, this working may well be the last-ever steam freight into Preston off the East Lancs line. Nevertheless, two engines have been out at Stansfield Hall on banking duties for most of the day; eventually returning to shed, No 48278 arriving first and then No 48191, both with chalked smokebox and tender inscriptions proclaiming 'Last Steam Copy Pit Banker 3rd August 1968'.

Other locos in steam on shed today are: 45156, 48348/93/519/715 with No 48773 (10F) being prepared for its railtour duty the following day and No 48519 (10F) being the standby engine.

In the Preston area, No 45318 (10D) starts its very busy final day at the head of 'Target 66'. It is seen in Farington Yard at 12:11 and then arriving back on Lostock Hall shed from the Bamber Bridge direction at 12:45 with diesel fuel tanks and coal wagons in tow.

Seen in steam on shed at various times today are: 44806/88/5073/110/212/60/305/18/88/407, 48476/723 (all 10D), 45156 Ayrshire Yeomanry, 45287, 48340/493 (all 10F), and 44781/871/4/94/5017, 70013 Oliver Cromwell, 73069 (all 10A). All the Carnforth engines and also Nos 45156, 45305 and 48476 are being prepared for railtours tomorrow. No 45156 has run light from Rose Grove, arriving at 17:15.

No 44806 (10D) has earlier worked a ballast train to/from an unidentified destination, and now arrives back on

working of all. The large complement of enthusiasts in the seven coaches are to have a poor run due to a succession of signal checks and, with stops being made at all stations from Kirkham, Blackpool South will be reached some 15 minutes late. Doubtless, the usually totally uninformed local press present will, in their inimitable manner, have a field day in apportioning the blame squarely on the steam locomotive.

An even larger number, however, has assembled for 1F51, the 21:25 to Liverpool Exchange, which is to be provided with No 45318 (10D) (which, it will be recalled, had earlier been shunting for most of the day on far more menial duties); the engine leaving shed again, coaled, watered and with a fresh crew, at 20:30 for Preston station. Word has somehow got around and a huge contingent of supporters has travelled to Preston to participate in this historic journey, which will be the

shed at 15:48. Its day's work is not complete, however, as it is required to go off shed again shortly before 19:30, light-engine to Preston station to present itself for station pilot/1A00 sleeping car heating duties. Half an hour later, No 45212 (10D) also slowly departs at 20:00, again light engine, to Preston station and will work 1P58, the 20:50 to Blackpool South - this being the penultimate steam passenger very last ordinary passenger train to be provided with steam haulage. The train itself is soon packed to capacity, the normally small number of ordinary passengers naturally wondering what on earth is going on. At the front end, driver Ernie Heyes and fireman Tony Smith soon provide some spirited running commensurate with the occasion and the journey is completed in a highly commendable time. What Ernie does not realise, until this is pointed out to him by fitter Pete Whalen upon the loco's return to the shed, is that, during the latter stages of the rapid dash across the South Lancashire plain, a hot box was sustained on one of the tender axles at probably some two miles out from Exchange station. It was fortunate indeed that this did not occur earlier in this historically very significant journey!

A more detailed account of the journeys of 1P58 and 1F51 is related elsewhere, but one the most significant aspects of these workings, for local enthusiasts, was in the actual selection of locomotives on the roster. Quite coincidentally, both engines had been 'local' (indeed, Fylde-based) engines for most of their existence. Very aptly, No 45212 was a Fleetwood engine

from 1948 until 1963 and No 45318 a Blackpool Central engine from 1955 to 1963.

Both trains carry headboards declaring 'The End' – the one on No 45318 being perhaps the most graphic in its impact. Upon return to Preston from Blackpool South – to date, the last steam engine ever to do so – No 45212 shunts the sleeping cars off the 23:45 Euston-Preston into the bay at Preston and this is very definitely the last occasion upon which passengers will be steam-hauled by a BR engine in normal service, albeit only during part of a shunt move!

Freight traffic everywhere being almost non-existent at weekends, Sunday 4 August 1968 is a far quieter day at all three depots, but particularly so at Carnforth and Rose Grove. Locos that had been in steam the previous day are still warm, with just a few pounds of steam pressure remaining, but, at Rose Grove, just two had a full head of steam. A very clean No 48773 is being prepared by Driver Arnold Hodgson and Fireman Jim Walker ready for the Blackburn to Carnforth, via Hellifield, leg of the LCGB 'Farewell to Steam Railtour' and a very grubby No 48519 had also been

LEFT On 2 August two engines have been out at Stansfield Hall on banking duties for most of the day; eventually returning to shed, No 48278 (seen here) arriving first and then No 48191, both with chalked smokebox and tender inscriptions proclaiming 'Last Steam Copy Pit Banker 3rd August 1968

In the very last light of a glorious day, an unidentified Rose Grove 8F crosses over the West Coast Main Line at Farington with 7N68, the 21:45 Preston NU Yard to Cudworth, which it will work as far as Rose Grove.

kept in steam, as standby for No 48773, just in case of any last minute failure. Perhaps not immediately apparant too many, No 48519 is the last LNER-built locomotive in BR service, constructed at Doncaster in 1944.

In 1958, Jim used to visit Rose Grove as a trainspotter and, in those less Health & Safety conscious days, often used to help the steam-raisers light up locos. On one particular occasion, he turned up to witness the incredulous sight of Arnold dressed in a suit and placing fires in locomotives himself! The steam-raiser had not turned-up for duty. Obviously Jim offered to help and

Arnold asked if he knew what to do? Jim answered, 'Yes', so Arnold took him over to the stores and told him to get what he needed, for himself. Between the two of them, they each took half of the shed - lighting up all the engines. That is what one might describe as a real enthusiast!

It is, therefore, all the more remarkable that today, all of ten years on, these two are once again sharing duties, now with the honour of crewing the very last Rose Grove steam engine to work a train. No 48773 eventually departs, accompanied by running shift Foreman Des Melia to the shed exit, and then proceeds light-engine towards Blackburn.

The only other crew booking on at Rose Grove on this Sunday are driver Alan Entwistle and his fireman Bob Ashworth, ready for a pw working in Rose Grove 'Up Grid' sidings in conjunction with the road bridge-renewal work over the station and yards. The turn has been booked for a 350hp diesel shunter (Class 08). Sensibly, rather than immediately drop the fire in No 48519, which has a full head of steam, it is decided to use the 8F on the pw job, to burn through the already very large fire. And so it falls to No 48519 and its crew

to be the last steam loco to leave Rose Grove shed… and to No 48773 to be the last steam loco to arrive on shed in the evening, upon its return light engine from Carnforth via Preston.

Over at Lostock Hall, No 48493 (10F) has found itself on shed with no further booked work on the Saturday evening. It will not return to Rose Grove, but is kept in steam until the following morning, as there is one final duty for it to undertake. Being seen in Farington Junction yard quietly shunting ballast wagons at 09:00 on the Sunday morning, this almost un-noticed and undocumented working is the very last non-passenger steam working on BR.

All the glory of the occasion obviously centres upon the various 'Farewell to Steam' specials; indeed, there has probably never before been such a concentration of workings of this nature in a single area, since there are no fewer than six steam-hauled trains touring Lancashire today. At Lostock Hall shed, the engine cleaners of the MNA have been busy. Indeed, this is their swan-song too – for after today there will be no more! Overnight, no less than an all-time record of 13 engines have been groomed in one session.

Replacement self-adhesive smokebox numerals or shed-plates have been applied and bufferbeams painted and the final curtain-call for steam stands in the yard in all its majesty, reflecting the early morning sunlight. For those who have laboured tirelessly through the night, before the very last steam chase begins, there is now time to cogitate on various successes achieved over the years. "Where will we be going tomorrow? What engines will we be cleaning?" is the question we would all love to be asking each other, for realisation still has to hit most of us. But, there is no escaping the inevitable… there is nothing beyond The End. Groups mill around aimlessly, perhaps looking for The Answer in each other, but there is none.

In ones and twos, throughout the morning the last men and machines gradually depart to their allocated rendezvous points, leaving a shed yard eerily empty and silent – for even the enthusiasts have now deserted their 'Mecca'.

Everyone has different recollections of that day and it is, perhaps, best to let the photographs in the following chapters tell their own stories. However, with the onset of evening, very few observers remain to witness the bitter end. By 22:00, there are 16 engines on shed in steam (not all, of course, having been used today) and with only Nos 70013 and 45156 still awaited back from specials' duty. Oliver Cromwell does finally materialise at some time after midnight, but No 45156 is, by far, the last engine of all to return. It is around 04:00 on the Monday morning when Driver Andy Hall backs his 'Black Five' onto a totally deserted shed. There is not another soul to be seen, so Andy's claim today to have been the very last steam footplateman on British Railways (11 August special events aside) appears to be justified.

Walking with his fireman in the eerie half-light down the serried ranks of now withdrawn engines, many still exuding their last ebbing signs of life, Andy proceeds into the engineman's lobby in order to sign-off duty, only to discover that the foreman's office has been ransacked, with even the two shed telephones having been ripped off the wall. The bodies of our dearly departed are not yet cold, but the vultures are already striking! Long live steam, for steam is dead!

Nightfall at Rose Grove. Chimneys, cooling towers, steam locomotives – everything visible in this evocative view has now disappeared forever. Indeed, a motorway now passes right through the middle of the picture, leaving but two sets of track leading towards Accrington.

Chapter 12

The final steam rosters
4 August 1968

The complete list of known motive power movements on this, the final day of steam, was as below:

10A Carnforth

48773 (10F) Light-engine 10A to 10F, after servicing off 1L50.
45390 (10A) & 45025 (10A) Light-engines 10D to 10A via WCML.

10D Lostock Hall

48493 (10F) 10D to Farington Jct Yard to shunt ballast wagons [09:00] and then back to 10D.
45156 (10F) Light-engine 10D to Longsight carriage sidings to collect stock for 1T80 and then return light Stockport (Edgeley) to 10D.

44871 (10A) & 44894 (10A) Light-engines 10D to Manchester (Vic) for 1Z78 [dep 10:37], then return light to 10D.
45390 (10A) & 45025 (10A) Light-engines 10D to Manchester (Vic) for 1Z74, then return light to 10A, via WCML.
44874 (10A) & 45017 (10A) Light-engines 10D to Manchester (Vic) for 1Z79 [dep 11:00], then return light to 10D.
48476 (10D) & 73069 (10A) Light-engines 10D to Manchester (Vic) for 1L50 [dep 10:40], then return light to 10D.
44781 (10A) & 70013 (10A) Light-engines 10D to Manchester (Vic) for 1Z74/1L50 [dep 11:49], then return to 10D.
45305 (10D) Light-engine 10D to Manchester (Vic) for 1T85, [dep 11:49] then return light to 10D.
45407 (10D) Light-engine 10D to Blackburn for 1L50 [dep 12:50], then

return light to 10D.

70013 (10A) Light-engine 10D to Manchester (Vic) for 1Z74 [dep 11:49] and light engine Blackburn to Lostock Hall for 1L50, return light to 10D.

10F Rose Grove

48519 (10F) Permanent way train shunt in Rose Grove 'Up' Sidings and then back to 10F.

48773 (10F) Light-engine Rose Grove MPD to Blackburn for 1L50, then return light 10A to 10F, after servicing.

The six railtours were as below:

(1T80) GC Enterprises 'Farewell to Steam Railtour'

(Starting/finishing point: Stockport (Edgeley) 8-coaches. Route: Stockport (Edgeley)-Denton-Droylesden-Manchester (Vic)-Bolton-Blackburn-Hellifield-Carnforth (rev)-Hellifield-Blackburn-Bolton-Manchester (Vic)-Droylesden-Denton-Stockport (Edgeley)

Motive power: Class 5MT 4-6-0 No 45156 Ayrshire Yeomanry (10D) throughout

Stockport to Blackburn: Driver Ronnie Clough (10D) / Fireman Joseph Booth (10D); Blackburn to Carnforth and return to Blackburn: Driver Colin Hacking / Fireman: Dennis Robinson; Blackburn to Stockport and LE to Lostock Hall: Driver Andy Hall (10D)

(1T85) British Railways 'Last Days of Steam' tour

(Starting/finishing point: Manchester (Vic)) 8-coaches Route: Manchester (Vic)-Eccles-Olive Mount-Bootle Branch-Birkdale-Southport avoiding line-Wigan (Wallgate)-Manchester (Vic)
Motive power: Class 5MT 4-6-0 No 45305 (10D) throughout
Man. Vic to Southport: Driver Vinny Commons (10D) / Fireman Paul Tuson (10D).

(1L50) Railway Correspondence & Travel Society 'End of Steam Commemorative Railtour'

(Starting/finishing point: London Euston) 13-coaches. Stage 1: Manchester (Vic)-Thorpes Bridge Jct-Oldham (Mumps)-Milnrow-Rochdale-Bury (Knowsley St)-Bolton-Blackburn

THE FINAL STEAM ROSTERS

```
                    LONDON MIDLAND REGION
     SPECIAL LOCOMOTIVES PROGRAMMES                    D262 S
                           ON DUTY 1725
LOSTOCK HALL                                   A. S. HALL
     SUNDAY 4 AUGUST
     DRIVER AND FIREMAN
          Lostock Hall        -        By bus
          Preston          18 25      As pass
     18 48 Blackburn
          RELIEVE 1T80 at 19 30
          Blackburn          19 34     1T80
     20 25 Manchester Vic.    20 30     1T80
     20 53 Stockport          21 10     ECS
     21 23 Longsight CS               LE/AR
          Lostock Hall MPD
                           45156        THE LAST STEAM ENGINE
```
— 2 AUG 1968 — LOSTOCK HALL

Motive power: Class 8F 2-8-0 No 48476 (10D) & Standard Class 5MT 4-6-0 No 73069 (10A) – double-headed
48476 Driver: Harry Bolton (10D) / Fireman: Jim Marlor (10D);
73069 Driver: John Burnett (10D) / Fireman: John Roach (10D)
Stage 2: Blackburn-Clitheroe-Hellifield (rev)-Skipton (reverse)-Colne-Accrington-Blackburn-Farington Jct.
Motive power: Class 5MT 4-6-0 No 45407 (10D) & Standard Class 5MT 4-6-0 No 73069 (10A) – double-headed
73069 Driver John Burnett (10D) / Fireman John Roach (10D);
45407 Driver: Fred Barron (10D)
Stage 3: Lostock Hall-Chorley-Bolton-Manchester (Vic)-Miles Platting-

Denton-Stockport (Edgeley) (Train scheduled to run via Burscough, Southport and Olive Mount, but diverted due to very late-running.
Motive power: Class 7MT 4-6-2 No 70013 Oliver Cromwell (10A)
Driver: Brian McFadden (10D) / Footplate Inspector: Frank Watson

(1Z74) Locomotive Club of Great Britain 'Farewell to Steam Railtour'

(Starting from London St Pancras and returning to London Euston) 12-coaches
Stage 1: Manchester (Vic)-Bolton (Trinity St)-Blackburn
Motive power: Class 7MT 4-6-2 No. 70013 Oliver Cromwell (10A) & Class 5MT 4-6-0 No 44781 (10A) – double-headed.
44781 Driver: Frank Herdman (10D) / Fireman: Eric Ashton (10D);
70013 Footplate Inspector: Frank Watson
Stage 2: Blackburn-Hellifield-Carnforth (rev)
Motive power: Class 8F 2-8-0 No 48773 (10F) & Class 5MT 4-6-0 No 44781 (10A) – double-headed
48773 Driver Arnold Hodgson / Fireman Jim Walker (10F)
Stage 3: Carnforth-Hellifield-Blackburn-

Farington Jct
Motive power: Class 5MT 4-6-0 No. 45390 (10A) & Class 5MT 4-6-0 No. 45025 (10A) – double-headed.

(1Z78) Stephenson Locomotive Society 'Farewell to Steam Railtour' - No 1

(Starting/finishing point: Birmingham New St) 10-coaches
Manchester (Vic)-Stalybridge-Huddersfield-Sowerby Bridge-Copy Pit-Blackburn-Bolton avoiding line-Wigan (Wallgate)-Kirkby-Bootle branch-Stanley-Rainhill-Eccles-Manchester (Vic)-Droylesden-Stockport (Edgeley)
Motive power: Class 5MT 4-6-0 No 44871 (10A) & Class 5MT 4-6-0 No 44894 (10A) – double-headed.
44871 Driver: Cliff Nelson (10D) /
Fireman: John Fletcher (10D);
44894 Driver: Ronnie Hall (10D) /
Fireman: Tom Jones (10D)

(1Z79) Stephenson Locomotive Society 'Farewell to Steam Railtour' - No 2

(Starting/finishing point: Birmingham New Street) 10-coaches
Manchester (Vic)-Stalybridge-Huddersfield-Sowerby Bridge-Copy Pit-

Blackburn-Bolton avoiding line-Wigan (Wallgate)-Kirkby-Bootle branch-Stanley-Rainhill-Eccles-Manchester (Vic)-Droylesden-Stockport (Edgeley)
Motive power: Class 5MT 4-6-0 No 44874 (10A) & Class 5MT 4-6-0 No 45017 (10A) – double-headed.
44874 Driver: John Commons (10D) /
Fireman: Roy Haythornthwaite (10D);
45017 Driver: Bill Wilson (10D)

Chapter 13

Farewell to Steam

4 August 1968

Steam enthusiasts had a field day on Sunday 4 August 1968, as six special train workings had been arranged to be steam-hauled within the boundaries of the Manchester and Preston Divisional Areas.

The Stephenson Locomotive Society organised two separate trains, 1Z78 and 1Z79, to run from Birmingham, via Manchester Victoria, to Huddersfield, returning via Copy Pit, Rose Grove, Blackburn, Bolton, Wigan and Rainford, where they were booked a 10-minute stop prior to the both of them returning to Manchester, via Earlestown and Kenyon Junction. The first special, 1Z78, departed Birmingham at 08:20, followed by 1Z79 at 09:05, and each was allowed time at Rose Grove so

that passengers could look around the motive power depot. If everything ran smoothly and the trains to time, it would still be almost 11 hours before they would arrive back at Birmingham (New Street).

The Railway Correspondence & Travel Society had arranged a special train (1L50) to run from Euston to Skipton that, after arriving at Manchester (Victoria), was scheduled for a trip via Rochdale, Castleton East Junction, Bury, Bolton, Blackburn and Hellifield, before arriving at Skipton. It was then booked to run via Colne, Blackburn, Lostock Hall, Ormskirk, Bootle Junction and Rainhill, before returning to Manchester via Earlestown and Kenyon Junction. This train comprised 13 coaches totalling 442 tons and, with engine No 70013 Oliver Cromwell and a Lostock Hall crew, I was scheduled to travel as inspector from Lostock Hall, via Rainhill, Manchester Victoria and then onwards to Stockport.

Meanwhile, the Locomotive Club of Great Britain had organised its own railtour (1Z74) from St Pancras to Carnforth which, after arriving at Manchester (Victoria), was scheduled a rather complicated route onwards to Carnforth. From Manchester (Victoria), it travelled via Bolton, Blackburn, Hellifield, Settle Junction and Wennington to Carnforth. It was booked to return by the same route to Blackburn and then by way of Lostock Hall Junction, before rejoining the West Coast Main Line at Farington Junction, to return home via Crewe. Upon arrival at Manchester (Victoria), I was then again rostered to accompany engine No 70013 with a set of Lostock Hall men, double-heading this train via Bolton and Walton Summit to Blackburn.

Another more-locally organised railtour (1T80) from Stockport to Carnforth, was operated by 'GC Enterprises', which, from Manchester (Victoria), followed the same route to Carnforth as 1Z74, but upon arrival

back at Blackburn, it then travelled via Darwen and Bolton back to Manchester and Stockport.

The final special train (1T85) was a BR London Midland Region railtour that had the title 'Last Days of Steam', but turned out to be a much less ambitious affair than any of the others, as it only went from Manchester to Southport and back, leaving Manchester Victoria at 14:20 and arriving back at 17:10.

When I arrived at Lostock Hall Shed on Sunday 4 August, at about 09:30, the place was a hive of activity, with numerous engines being prepared to work various stages of the aforementioned specials. Official railway personnel on duty proved to be totally outnumbered both by enthusiasts and other members of the public merely wanting to witness the passing of an era. Some of the enthusiasts had certainly been busy during the night, as they had attempted to make every engine look its best for this, the very last curtain-call for steam.

After watching No 70013 being prepared, I noticed that the engine sported the wooden mock nameplates that seemed to be fitted whenever the engine worked trains organised by the RCTS. According to our engine workings, we were booked off shed at 11:49 and to travel to Manchester light-engine coupled to a 'Black Five', then to work as assistant engine on 1Z74 (the LCGB tour to Carnforth), between Manchester Victoria and Blackburn, departing Manchester Victoria at 13:30 and arriving at Blackburn at 14:22, that is, if everything was running to time. On arrival at Blackburn, after hooking-off, we were timed to run light-engine back to Lostock Hall, in order to be re-manned, before working another enthusiasts' special, 1L50, (RCTS) from Lostock Hall later in the day.

To say that things did not go well would be a gross understatement, as, for a variety of reasons, most of the special trains failed to keep to their booked timings.

We left Lostock Hall shed on time at 11:49, with nothing to delay us en-route. 1Z74 itself, however, eventually ran into Manchester Victoria nearly an hour late and we then experienced further delays at Bolton due to Sunday engineering works. After Bolton, we did enjoy a clear run up the bank to Walton Summit and then down into Blackburn, and, with a load of only nine coaches totalling 314 tons, little effort was required from the two engines as we tried to pull back a bit of the lost time. After hooking-off at Blackburn, we then ran light-engine as scheduled tender-first back to Lostock Hall Shed, via a reversal at Todd Lane Junction Station. This saved turning the engine on the shed for the next stage of our tour of duty. At 16:30, No 70013, now with the fresh set of locomen, was then scheduled to work 1L50 from Lostock Hall Station to Stockport, via Burscough Jct, Ormskirk, Aintree and Rainhill, before returning via St Helens Jct and Earlestown to Manchester Victoria - where we were booked to take water. As was to transpire, by this time the special was running about four hours late and when it did eventually arrive at Lostock Hall, in order to attempt to regain some time, a decision had been taken by the RCTS officials to request Preston Control to permit the special to take a more direct route home. In the event the train took the 'back line' from Lostock Hall Jct to Farington Jct and then ran via Chorley and Bolton to Manchester.

We had a reasonable run from Lostock Hall Jct, but, with a load of all of 13 coaches behind the tender, only a little time could be recovered. To make matters worse, upon our arrival at Manchester Victoria, we discovered that there was no water available from our platform column. A decision now had to be made - should the train be delayed further, by detaching the engine, to source out a supply of water, or should we press on regardless to Stockport? The water-level gauge on the tender tank indicated that we had just below 1000 gallons remaining but, being familiar with the engine, I was aware that this gauge was 'shy', thus intimating that there was always slightly more water in the tender than appeared to be the case. I also climbed onto the tender and shone a 'Bardic' lamp into the tank, before then making the decision to continue to Stockport.

Instead of arriving there at the booked time of 18:56, we were still about 3½ hours late and darkness had already descended on the station. As we were hooking-off to seek that urgently needed refreshment, a mock coffin was being transported down the platform – a token gesture to signify the death of steam traction on British Railways. What moved me most of all, as we pulled away light engine, were the shouts of "Will ye no come back again?" Due to the efforts, particularly of the staff on the Great Central Railway, the wishes of those rail enthusiasts of many years ago have since become reality.

For the passengers on 1L50, they later had the rare privilege of having part of their fare - £1-2s-0d (£1.10) - returned as an offer of 'compensation'. By the time that their train had arrived back at Euston, it was just before 02:00 on the Monday morning - a mere four hours after booked time! Nevertheless, British Railways could not offer the weather as an excuse, as this had been fine and sunny all day long... but, at least the thousands of photographers lining the various routes to record the events enjoyed their day, as conditions had been ideal for them.

To complete the tale, fortunately we did manage to obtain water at Stockport, before proceeding tender-first back to Lostock Hall shed. For myself, I could now make my weary way homewards in the direction of Accrington, for a well-earned rest!

Frank Watson
Acting Footplate Inspector
(British Railways 1951-1970)

Chapter 14

"Last sunrise for steam"

Lostock Hall shed 4 August 1968

The final dawn for the condemned. A view taken from the top of the Lostock Hall coaling plant, this historically important photograph depicts the last curtain-call of all for steam standing in the yard in all its majesty. All the glory of the occasion obviously centres upon the various 'Farewell to Steam' specials; indeed, there has probably never before been such a concentration of workings of this nature in a single area, since there are no fewer than six steam-hauled trains touring Lancashire today. Rows of immaculate locos reflecting the early morning sunlight, the engine cleaners of the MNA have obviously been busy. Indeed, this is their swansong too – for after today there will be no more! Overnight, no less than an all-time record of 13 engines have been groomed in one session.

No 70013 is prepared at Lostock Hall shed, prior to running light to Manchester Victoria. Alongside is No 45110, which had been the rostered loco to take over from 8F No 48476 at Blackburn on 1L50, the RCTS special. However, someone in the BR hierarchy had then decreed that a standby loco should be sent to Manchester for 1T85, and the depot foreman had then selected the equally immaculate and fully lined-out No 45110. The latter, being sent light to Manchester, stood there all day doing nothing, before then returning to the shed – a complete waste of a superb locomotive.

Replacement self-adhesive smokebox numerals and shedplates have been applied, bufferbeams repainted, fires banked up, tenders refilled and all that is now needed is for the crews to book on duty. In ones and twos, throughout the morning the last men and machines will gradually depart to their allocated rendezvous points, leaving a shed yard eerily empty and silent.

Lostock Hall fireman Jim Marlor prepares to leave shed with 8F No 48476, coupled to No 73069, running light to Manchester Victoria, where both engines will stand to await the arrival from London of the RCTS special.

48476

Driver Frank Herdman, a recent transfer from Stockport with the end of steam at 9B, is the booked driver for today's itinerary for No 70013. The loco has a busy day in front of it, for, at different times, it will later be seen at the head of both an LCGB and an RCTS special and, here, Frank is seen awaiting the two 'Black Fives' that will accompany him light-engine to Manchester Victoria.

70013

Lostock Hall fitter Tommy Baldwin passes a replica wooden Oliver Cromwell nameplate up to fitter Pete Whelan ready to affix to the smoke deflector of No 70013.

For some the time has already come. No 44878, never a popular engine at 10D, ever since it first arrived from Kingmoor, is totally ignored by the cleaners and has already been dumped on No 10 Road to await its inevitable destiny,"

For those who have laboured tirelessly through the night, before the very last steam chase begins, there is now time to cogitate on various successes achieved over the years. "Where will we be going tomorrow? What engines will we be cleaning?" is the previously much-exclaimed question that, even today, is still on most of our lips… for full realisation has yet to hit us. Nevertheless, there is no escaping the inevitable… there is nothing beyond The End. As crews arrive and prepare their allocated steeds, discarded ladders and tins of cleaning oil lie around and, some still with cleaning rags in their hands, our group mills around aimlessly, perhaps looking for The Answer in each other. But none is forthcoming.

Chapter 15

My final steam turn

Former Lostock Hall fireman, Paul Tuson, recalls his own involvement in the events of 4 August 1968

On 4 August 1968, I was rostered at 10D Lostock Hall shed as the fireman to work on British Railways' own 'Last Days of Steam' tour (1T85). One of six enthusiasts' special trains running on this, the very last day of steam, my booked locomotive was to be one of the ubiquitous Stanier 'Black Five' 4-6-0s based here, No 45305, and my driver was to be no less than Vinny Commons, a colleague with whom I always found it a real pleasure to work. We booked on together at 10:49 and set to preparing our locomotive for its last moments of glory.

Always one of the externally visually more presentable of the 'Black Fives' on the shed's allocation, No 45305 was also one of the 13 locos that had just previously received a thorough polishing overnight by a group of clandestine engine cleaners.

Light engine to Manchester

All the other locos having departed during the morning to their respective rendezvous points, at around noon we coupled up to No 70013 Oliver Cromwell and another 'Black Five', No 44781, and the three of us then set off to proceed light engine towards Manchester. In so doing, the following weekend's event apart, we were probably the last departure from our shed of locomotives still in normal service.

Upon arrival at Victoria station, it

The roster-board in the lobby at Lostock Hall shed, for the six specials on the final day, 4 August 1968, in fact originally did not show No 45305 allocated to the duty that it eventually came to work. The actual engine selected by the shed had been No 45407. On Friday 26 July, a local enthusiast had arranged for No 45305 to be put on 6P16, the 18:15 Ribble Sidings-Carnforth. However, it was removed from that job and No 45212 appropriated instead. When asked for a reason why, it was advised that BR wanted it specially preparing for their special on 4 August and the '15 Guinea Special' the following weekend. No 45305 was, therefore, washed out during the coming week, thoroughly cleaned and put aside, doing nothing further all week. Meanwhile, No 45110 had been the rostered loco to take over from No 48476 at Blackburn on 1L50, the RCTS special. However, someone in the BR hierarchy had then decreed that a standby loco should be sent to Manchester for 1T85, and whoever it was that was on duty at 10D had then selected the equally immaculate and fully lined-out No 45110. No 45110 being sent light to Manchester, stood there all day doing nothing, before returning to the shed. In actual fact, No 45305's own booked job had originally been to pilot No 73069 on 1L50, the RCTS special, from Blackburn to Skipton and then back to Farington Junction. As 1T85 was the special organised by BR itself, very clearly, some strings must have been pulled at a high level of management, for some last-minute changes were made and the very unkempt (and uncleaned) standby engine, No 45407, came to be appropriated for 1L50.

was then up to Cheetham Hill carriage sidings, where we turned the engine, before coupling up to our stock waiting for us there. At around 13:45, we dropped the eight-vehicle ECS down the bank to pick up the patiently waiting passengers. The route our special was to take was Manchester (Victoria)-Eccles-Earlestown-Bootle branch-Birkdale-Southport (Chapel Street) avoiding line-Wigan (Wallgate)-Dobbs Brow and back to Manchester (Victoria).

Due to the exceptionally late-running of the RCTS special from London, which was forced to truncate its itiner-ary, the tour was the only one that day to cover the section of line where the original locomotive trials were held by the Liverpool and Manchester Railway in 1829 and Parkside, where the Rt Hon William Huskisson MP was killed following the official opening ceremony in 1830.

Two footplate passengers

Upon drawing to a stand in Platform 11 Middle (the long one connecting Victoria with Exchange), we were joined by two footplate passengers,

MY FINAL STEAM TURN

RIGHT 70013
Oliver Cromwell.
Loughborough engine
sheds, May 2008.
Its amazing how
much effort the team
at Loughborough
have put in to get
this loco back to
steaming again.

one being a local conductor-driver (my driver didn't know the road between Manchester and Liverpool, it not being a route normally worked by Lostock hall men) and the other being a rather surly character whose identity we never did discover. Whether he was a footplate inspector, or perhaps some other higher-up official, was unclear, but he did, nevertheless, produce a valid footplate pass.

Right away

Anyway, at around 14:20 we got the 'right-away' and set off along the ex-LNWR line towards Liverpool. No 45305 was steaming well and we soon arrived at Olive Mount Junction, just short of Edge Hill, where our conductor alighted, to be replaced by another man to pilot us onwards towards Southport.

Having turned right at Olive Mount off the direct route down into Lime Street, we then proceeded along the, by now, goods-only line through Stanley and Tue Brook, to gain access near Bootle onto the Liverpool Exchange to Southport third-rail dc electric line.

Not unsurprisingly, there were a few surprised faces hereabouts, for the locals had long become accustomed to seeing EMUs - and not a steam locomotive and 'real' coaches! Indeed, no regular steam passenger workings had passed this way since the through Southport-Euston coaches, normally hauled by 2-6-4 tanks as far as Lime Street, had ceased running some years previously.

At Southport, our second pilot driver alighted, at last permitting the ever-patient Vinny to take over at the controls. We managed a quick dash over the racing stretch of mainly level track of the ex-L&Y route through Burscough Bridge, before coming to a stand at Wigan (Wallgate), in order to take a, supposedly, 10-minute stop for water.

Water supply problems

Having not been used for a while, the bag at the column was leaking badly and this operation was clearly going to take quite some time. Indeed, the tank was filling so slowly, that a decision was soon made to uncouple No 45305 from our stock and to cross over to the opposite platform to fill up there. This move proved to be a sensible one and, eventually, we were able to back up again onto the train.

It was at this point that our 'mystery' passenger assured me that he would 'put a fire on' for the steep climb up to Hindley, however he made no immediate move to do so and, after waiting for a while in anticipation, I eventually had to pick up the shovel to 'gas her up' myself. We had to set off shortly after this and, unfortunately, the fire that I had just put on hadn't had chance to burn through properly.

Nevertheless, off went Vinny, steam pressure and water level both falling steadily, as he hammered No 45305 up the bank with full regulator and probably 40 to 50 per cent cut-off. I decided to give the fire a good root through with the pricker to help it along. This produced plenty of black smoke and would be described in the Handbook for Steam Locomotive Enginemen as 'incomplete combustion', but it did produce the required effect and we did eventually top the bank, where the road fortunately eased to permit an uneventful run along the direct line via Crows Nest and Dobbs Brow Junctions back to Victoria and back to Lostock Hall.

For an outlay of a mere £2-0s-0d, passengers had been treated to almost three hours of steam haulage and after all the final photographs had been taken, we took the empty stock back up the

bank to Cheetham Hill carriage sidings. As far as Vinny and I were concerned, the day was not quite yet over, for we still had to turn the loco again, before setting off light engine all the way back to Lostock Hall shed. As we booked off duty, so ended our last job with steam and, at the time, we thought the end had also come for No 45305. But that, of course, is quite another story!

Chapter 16

The last day specials
4 August 1968

Having endured an extended station stop to take on water, the spotlessly cleaned and fully lined-out Class 5MT No 45305 storms up the bank out of Wigan Wallgate, on the former L&Y main line from Liverpool to Manchester, with the British Railways-organised 'Last Days of Steam' railtour of 4 August 1968.

Lydgate Viaduct, on the Todmorden to Burnley route via Copy Pit. The first of two Stephenson Locomotive Society specials passes over, double-headed by 'Black Five' 4-6-0s No 44871 with driver Cliff Nelson and fireman John Fletcher and No 44894 with driver Ronnie Hall and fireman Tom Jones - an all Lostock Hall crewing!

With an unusually matching set of blue and grey stock (perhaps borrowed for the day from Longsight depot and from its more usual workings to Euston) No 45156 passes over the western end of the local beauty spot at Entwistle Reservoir.

Working apparently flat-out, the second SLS special storms up the last few yards to Copy Pit summit and, once again, there is an all Lostock Hall crew on board. Motive power is also again 'Black Five' 4-6-0s, this time, No 44874 with driver John Commons and fireman Roy Haythornthwaite and No 45017 with driver Bill Wilson and fireman Billy Bamber.

THE GRAND FINALE OF BRITISH STEAM

Heading up the hill at Turton, the RCTS special is in charge of yet another Lostock Hall crew. 8F 2-8-0 No 48476 with driver Harry Bolton and fireman Jim Marlor, double-heads Standard 5MT 4-6-0 No 73069 with driver John Burnett and fireman John Roach.

Literally yards further on Nos 48476 and 73069 are captured yet again, on the climb up to Sough Tunnel. The line climbs at gradients as steep as 1-in-73 for the first six miles out of Bolton and in earlier times many freight trains were banked along this stretch.

At Blackburn, the 8F was removed from the RCTS special and replaced by 'Black Five' No 45407 for the remainder of the journey to Carnforth. Here, driver Fred Barron looks out as the train climbs to Wilpshire Summit.

Chapter 17

Motive power arrangements

11 August 1968

10 August 1968
Light engine Carnforth-Lostock Hall
Motive power: Class 7MT 4-6-2 No 70013 Oliver
Cromwell (10A)
Footplate Inspector: Frank Watson

11 August 1968
Light engine: Lostock Hall-Liverpool Lime Street
Motive power: Class 5MT 4-6-0 No 45110 (10D)
Unknown crew
Light engines: Carnforth-Hellifield (reverse)-Carlisle
Motive power: Class 5MT 4-6-0 No 44871 (10A) &
Class 5MT 4-6-0
No 44781 (10A) – double-headed. 44871 - Driver:
Willie Pape (ex-Carlisle man) / Fireman: John
Gorst (both of 10A) / Acting Loco Inspector: Frank
Watson. 44781 - Driver: Charlie Wilson / Fireman:

Jeff Beattie (both of 10A) / Loco Inspector: Bert
Moore (Carnforth)

**1T57 the British Railways-organised 'Fifteen
Guinea Special'**
Liverpool (Lime Street) to Carlisle and return: 10
coaches

**Stage 1: Liverpool Lime Street-Earlestown-
Manchester Victoria**
Motive power: Class 5MT 4-6-0 No 45110 (10D)
Driver: Jack Hart (8A) / Fireman: Brian Bradley (8A)

**Stage 2: Manchester Victoria-Bolton-Blackburn
Hellifield-Settle-Carlisle**
Motive power: Class 7MT 4-6-2 No 70013 Oliver
Cromwell (10A)

Driver from Man. Vic to Blackburn: Unknown /
Fireman: Tommy Gorman (Preston). Driver from
Blackburn to Carlisle: Bob Grogan / Fireman:
Raymond Watton. Guard: John Weal / Loco
Inspector: Chief Inspector John Hughes

Stage 3: Carlisle-Settle-Hellifield-Blackburn.
Motive power: Class 5MT 4-6-0 No 44871 (10A) &
Class 5MT 4-6-0. No 44781 (10A) - double-headed.
44871 - Driver: Norman Ashton / Fireman: Tony
Helm / Loco Inspector: Chief Inspector John Hughes.
44781 - Driver: Ray Grimshaw / Fireman:
David Greenhalgh / Loco Inspector: Bert Moore
(Carnforth)

**Stage 4: Blackburn-Bolton-Manchester Victoria,
Light Engine direct to Carnforth**
Motive power: Class 5MT 4-6-0 No 44871 (10A) &
Class 5MT 4-6-0. No 44781 (10A) – double-headed.
44871 - Driver: Ted Fothergill (10A) / Fireman:
Malcolm Thistlethwaite (10A) / Loco Inspector
to Manchester: Chief Inspector John Hughes.
44781 - Driver: Jack Simpson (10A) / Fireman: Ian
Thistlethwaite (10A) / Loco Inspector: Bert Moore
(Carnforth)

**Stage 5: Manchester Victoria-Earlestown-
Liverpool Lime Street**
Motive power: Class 5MT 4-6-0 No 45110 (10D)
Driver: Fred Smith (8A) / Fireman: Stephen Roberts
(8A) / Loco Inspector: John Hughes.

**Light engine: Liverpool Lime Street-Wigan-
Lostock Hall**
Motive power: Class 5MT 4-6-0 No 45110 (10D)
Unknown crew
**Light engine: Carlisle-Settle-Hellifield-
Blackburn-Lostock Hall**
Motive power: Class 7MT 4-6-2 No 70013 Oliver
Cromwell (10A)
Driver from Carlisle to Blackburn: Bob Grogan /
Fireman: Raymond Whatton / Acting Footplate
Inspector: Frank Watson (Carlisle-Lostock Hall-
Accrington)
**Light engine: Loco went onto Lostock Hall depot
for servicing and then straight to Norwich via
Doncaster** - Healey Mills crew Motive power: Class
7MT 4-6-2 No 70013 Oliver Cromwell (32A)

'The Fifteen Guinea Special' - the last British Railways steam
hauled train en route from Manchester Victoria to Liverpool Lime
Street hauled by LMS 5MT 4-6-0 45110.

Chapter 18

IT57 - Aboard the train

11 August 1968

I'd never been an ardent railtour sup-porter (having been a passenger on only four between late 1965 and 1T57) because of cost and a devotion to 'nor-mal service' steam. Though tempted by 1T57, I'd admittedly, baulked at the fare, but it was my mum who, surpris-ingly, persuaded me to 'lash out' and travel, because she knew what those years of following BR steam, to the 'nth degree', meant to me. I think her gesture was fuelled by relief that it was all over and a hope that her son would now begin to lead the life of a normal 19-year-old!

Lostock Hall shed proved to be the base for Sunday's tour engines. We went to have a look on Saturday morning, but after noting only

Nos 45110 and 45305 (both 10D) newly fired, were ejected in no uncer-tain way! There'd doubtless been lots of enthusiasts, partly at a loose-end, trying to get round Lostock Hall that day and, by noon, the staff were clearly fed up with it all. Part of that very warm afternoon, I watched the summer Saturday go busily by at Preston station, then returned home (loco-hauled) to prepare for the 11th.

No train from Bolton on Sunday would have got me to Liverpool in time. My dad would, doubtless, have obliged with a lift, but it wasn't worth risking even the remotest chance of a delay or breakdown, with so much (let alone the 15 guineas!) at stake. So, I was there by train mid-Saturday evening.

Pictures of Lime Street, showing No

45110, simply adorned with its 1T57 board, the train seemingly hemmed in by countless onlookers filling every available inch of platform and more, yet kept tidily in check by a single visible policeman, are most easily brought to mind by most enthusiasts. My designated seat was at the train's very rear on that first leg to Manchester, so I quickly grabbed a RH drop window in the brake next to the engine.

BR had intended to cater for 470 passengers, but from the surprisingly varied reports that followed, 420 would seem to have been the sum total of tickets sold, but more of the press anon. One minute late, I made it, 5110 with its train of 10 coaches, 3641/2 tons net, began the very difficult cold start at 09:11, paced briefly, as intended, by the electrically hauled 09:10 to Euston. This pulled ahead quickly, as No 45110, after several slips, plugged away against the

1-in-93 to Edge Hill, attaining 14mph towards the top. It wasn't at all easy, but Jack Hart, the 61-year-old driver now passing close to his old shed would have known what to expect; 59mph followed a check at Edge Hill No 4, but six minutes had been lost to Rainhill, the first commemorative halt.

Cutting down that photographic stop to eight minutes among a sea of freely wandering spectators and passengers was a wonder challenged only by my joining them and returning to find my all-important window still free! On time away, 63mph preceded checks up to, and a halt at, Parkside, to commemorate the unfortunate fatality there in steam's infancy. Though 1T57 made no inroads into the new, but slight arrears, 5110 sounded in fine form chattering across Barton Moss, with such an even exhaust that it could have been a Caprotti. We were up to 63 before Patricroft, then a bad slowing after Eccles put the tour seven late into Victoria.

If we believe the shortlist of locos originally advised by BR, No 45110 had not been under consideration, unless, as I strongly suspect, No 45310 appeared only due to a misprint. Any other misplaced digit would have thrown up a non-existent or long withdrawn loco, thereby eliminating conjecture.

As the morning warmed up outside, I walked back to claim my premier window seat for the next 125¾ miles, immediately behind the engine, on the left and facing too! The generous half-hour allowance at Victoria, again with platforms crammed to the very edges, permitted No 70013 Oliver Cromwell to get away only a minute late, but the difficult Platform 14 start wasn't to the Pacific's liking. It slipped time and time again (17 on my recording), but once onto the straight, in true 'Belfast Boat Train' style, leapt ahead, comparatively. 44mph over Agecroft Jct fell to a steady 40 on to Farnworth, marginally improving before we threaded Bolton at close to the prescribed limit, having lost no further time.

I recorded the whole ascent from Bradshawgate Box to Walton's Sidings. The reason that my left arm ached considerably in the closing stages was the 21-minute duration of that climb, the features of which, to any 'first time southerners' would have been handsomely exaggerated. No 70013 started reasonably, but never behaved like a true Class 7 anywhere, in fact, and I can only presume either a persistent, but not serious, shortage of steam on the climb in question, or a degree of brake-drag'.

Maybe the valves were in need of attention, even. But, still, the engine remained entertaining, the 'Brit's' sharp, percussive blast never deserting it. From 23mph at The Oaks, we began to flag from Bromley Cross, really, experiencing a very gradual drop to 14mph at worst, just before Entwistle. Walton's Sidings stopped the train briefly and mysteriously, unless the cautious descent that followed was linked to some verbal message communicated to the crew. 1T57 nevertheless pulled into Blackburn on time, thanks to the unexacting schedule so far.

Due to difficulties watering, No 70013 had to come off the train for that purpose, delaying its departure by half an hour, to the delight of journalists waiting for an irregularity to pounce on.

After some curious playing about with the regulator in the tunnel, our driver wisely decided that a generous opening was best to produce the

exciting staccato exhaust we heard so clearly on the climb to Cemetery Hill, surmounted at 36mph.

Since the first call at Walton's, just prior to midday, the stewards had experienced some problems in persuading those standing to sit down for lunch

Rainhill - 11 August 1968. A scene such as this would, in 2008, cause apoplexy in certain quarters! Given the sea of freely and aimlessly wandering spectators and passengers, it is little short of a miracle that the scheduled photographic stop is reduced to a mere eight minutes.

and clearing the tables of equipment for setting. It was good to see that the taking-in of the steam was uppermost in the minds of passengers other than me. The 'trimmings' on this tour were of little importance, personally, and I turned down the wine offered.

Sixty-four mph down through Langho helped a fairly swift run on to Hellifield and the 'Brit' had sustained 31mph up Rimington bank, again with a lot of gusto. We'd kept the booking from Blackburn, but water was also deemed necessary at Hellifield, though six minutes only were required for this. A very businesslike start to Long Preston (48mph) preceded an easing until Settle Jct, which could have been taken faster

than at 58. At about this stage in the journey we were informed that the souvenir scrolls which were being given out, had not been pre-inscribed with the recipient's name, as intended, and would have to be self-signed.

Thankfully, for the few making tape-recordings from the open stock, unwanted sounds were kept to a minimum. The clinking of plates and the like could hardly be objected to and it even added a degree of authentic class, as the train settled down to 32-35mph on the long climb to Blea Moor, where, if I may juxtapose two parts of commentary from an LP record made of the event soon after, "Even the lonely moorland that skirts the tracks at Ribblehead was crammed to the doors." Things did get a bit fraught in that locale personally, as I tried to cope with a tape wrap-round, log the run and have my lunch served (two hours after that first call), all at the same time.

It was a friend that later disclosed to me a 'disaster' of his own there. While I'd been struggling to disentangle the twisted tape, he, by the lineside had, in the excitement, forgotten to plug in his microphone!

It was indeed a glorious day for train-watching. Bare legs dangled from walls, even disused platform-edges and other vantage points, as the public turned out in force to wave and cheer us on our way. Morecambe secured the day's sunshine record of 13.2 hours, but it was no less summery elsewhere, even in those fells. Two thousand cars an hour were reported to have been entering Blackpool, but the few byways of Ais Gill were far more inconvenienced by perhaps a tenth of that.

We had been able to omit the booked water stop of five minutes at Blea Moor, but dropped 4mph in two minutes from that signalbox to entering the tunnel at 29mph. A photo-stop lined-up for Ais Gill was cut by five minutes too.

At least the journey continued to be remarkably free of engineering work for a Sunday and No 70013 managed unhindered progress from Ais Gill to Carlisle in 55 minutes. Top speeds of 75 at Ormside and 69 through Little Salkeld were still not fast enough, in view of our lateness and the 51-minute schedule, and we arrived 34 late.

The stop at Carlisle, more than halved to a quarter of an hour, took me unawares and still in my seat at what now was the train's rear. I was to blame and soon paid for my tardiness. Even a futile and largely obstructed walk through ten coaches and back looking for a free window didn't justify a 28-minute gap in my log almost to Culgaith!

The pair of 'Black Fives,' Nos 44781 piloted by 44871, were running very well. Emitting mostly a thin grey exemplary exhaust, they were clearly not to be trifled with, gaining five minutes to pass Appleby in just less than 40 at 60mph, after much speeding in the mid-60s. An unfortunate lapse to 36mph by Griseburn, ending the first 1-in-100 stretch, kept the Appleby to Ais Gill average down to a shade under 50mph, but a lively enough 52 over the summit made amends.

Quickly up to 70 over the crest, 1T57 swept round the curves approaching Garsdale at slightly less. Only a slack at Dent really prevented an on-time arrival at the Blea Moor water stop. This was extended to a photo opportunity too, but though descending to the ballast using the steps provided, I stayed at the train's rear, more peacefully obtaining an alternative view and also a shot of the signalbox, recalling, no doubt, the April afternoon spent therein more than two years previously and how so much more than the weather contrasted that day from this. We were away again at 16:21, breaking the thread of any such reverie.

Much less taxed in other departments than on the northbound run, I cheerfully accepted a spare 'high tea' salad, as well as my own, before Blackburn. The day's highest speed of 77mph came briefly approaching Settle, but the 17-minute lateness from Blea Moor was deviated from but a little through to Manchester. Our pair of 5MTs fell from 42mph through Whalley to 37 on the bank by Langho prior to a short signal stop at Wilpshire.

At Blackburn I walked forward again to tape our ascent to Walton's, being loath to let those classic uphill miles, of which I'd become so fond and familiar, slip by unrecorded, but window occupancy, as expected, prevented full absorption of the live event, to say the least. Through the early sunny evening we forged in the mid-30s, an urgent enough exhaust audible from one or both locos intermittently, until their exertions ceased at 31mph over the see-saw summit to which I never expected to return.

Uneventful was the rest of the running, with our double header, as the many familiar features on home ground were passed by, never to be seen again in quite the same way. Thoughts, until now largely distracted by goings on of the day spent steam hauled through town and country, began to turn to the significance of those diminishing miles.

1T57 halved the loco-changing allowance at Victoria to one of only seven minutes. This involved No 45110 coupling to our rear for the final (non-stop) stretch to Liverpool Lime Street. This time I couldn't be caught out by the slick operation!

The 4-6-0 began slowly, very slowly, but more sure-footedly than the Pacific, from Platform 12. It did feel as if the brake drag characteristics, real or imagined, had returned briefly. However, 5110 got away soon after, to hold very similar rates along the flat as it had that morning. A check before Newton we had, then the last highlight in sound with an energetic attack on the short but steep length of railway between St. Helens Jct and Rainhill.

As the lowering sun's rays of that beautiful summer's day played along and through the coach windows of our unnamed farewell train, they were metaphorically setting on so much more, a plain fact that few passengers, as 1T57 rolled its last miles into the city, were not deeply conscious of.

At a few seconds to 20:00, No 45110 came to rest at the Lime Street buffers. After collecting my belongings, I stood alone for some time opposite the familiar engine's smokebox, half lost to melancholy thought.

I still went home on the train from Liverpool, probably too late to catch Flying Scotsman's non-stop May ECML run on BBC TV (in colour). Maybe I'd shunned it in anticipation of continued inaccurate media representation.

There was plenty of that next morning, as people showed me four newspaper accounts of the 'Fifteen Guinea

ABOVE In the open countryside on the original Liverpool & Manchester Railway, No 45110 leaves a short tunnel near Kenyon Village

Special', two of which I'd dismissed as 'rubbish'. Ill-informed statements such as confusing the day's mileage with the number of passengers were mixed with over emphasis on cost and the leaving behind of careless journalists at stops, which had been shortened to reduce the lateness they also criticised! The Daily Express's Alan Bennett at least combined dignity with some useful information in his account. "WHAT A GLORIOUS WAY TO END IT ALL" read the headline. Yes, it had been indeed!

Steve Leyland

Chapter 19

IT57 - From the lineside
11 August 1968

The very last two regular BR standard gauge steam-hauled passenger service trains having departed, within minutes of each other, from adjacent platforms of Preston station on the evening of 3 August 1968, there were six special passenger and a solitary ballast working the following day that provided the final duties with steam for many of the crews at my local depot, 10D Lostock Hall.

THAT, as far as most ardent followers of steam in the late 1960s were concerned, really was THE END – a fact that had, indeed, been so poignantly proclaimed on the headboard of our shed's

No 45318, which I had photographed, surrounded by massive crowds, standing at the buffer-stops of Liverpool's

Exchange station the previous evening. After nearly a century and a half of loyal service of steam to the nation, it was all over – there would be no more! Not REAL steam, anyway.

Following hot on the heels of the announcement of a firm date for the death knell for the last three existing steam sheds, feelings were already running high in some quarters when it was not too long before the news also emerged that, despite nothing at all being planned for the redundant footplate crews themselves, the BRB had made the incredulous further disclosure that it was to organise a high profile final event after all, this to occur a mere seven days after the disposing of literally hundreds of its loyal steam men, many of whom had devoted their lives to

1T57 coasts effortlessly downhill over Smardale Viaduct, the highest viaduct on the S&C railway, towering 131ft over Scandal Beck and built entirely of grey limestone. Although not visible in this view, the trackbed of the closed Kirkby Stephen to Tebay line passes underneath the viaduct.

the railways. Some schools of thought considered the insensitive timing to be in extremely bad taste, but whatever the pros and cons of any reasoned argument, certainly such an occasion would somewhat tone-down or divert away from public awareness some of the more embarrassing aspects of how the steam infrastructure and its personnel did actually come to be disposed of.

Many critics of the plans became quite incensed, developing arguably jaundiced views that in all of this the railway societies in particular had perhaps received a raw deal or been cheated in some way. Whether a blatant display of one-upmanship or not, it was also contended that the BRB had taken unfair advantage in making such a move. Potentially, '1T57' came to present a real threat to carefully-made plans to operate the 4 August 'Last Day' specials (which, technically now, wouldn't be operating on the 'last day'

Journey's end - the border citadel of Carlisle. No 70013 awaits detaching from the train. Arrival at being some 30min late, the station-time is cut down to about 15 minutes and 'Black Fives' Nos 44781 and 44871 are already backing onto the other end ready for 1T57 to retrace its route back to Liverpool.

after all!). Although, for very valid operational reasons, just about every tour organiser in previous months had been permitted only to use steam on a severely restricted number of routes (these, essentially, within the environs of Lancashire), the major selling-point for this one was that the final working would traverse that 'Jewel in the Crown' of lines – the Settle & Carlisle Railway – AND in each direction - AND with steam all the way!

In an attempt to place a more-balanced perspective to any argument, others pointed out, perhaps unconvincingly, that surely, ANY steam action must be welcome to a steam enthusiast and, even though we all had a love/hate relationship with BR at some stage during the closing years of steam, it was, after all, trying to run a business and at a profit.

Nevertheless, whatever direction one's views tended to favour, it was an inescapable fact that, in 1968, £15.15s.0d - or 15 guineas - the asking price for a ticket to ride on the train - was more than the weekly wage of many working men. It was this aspect above all else that caused many also to accuse BR of unfair profiteering – despite the undoubtedly high costs involved in setting up such an event. But, conversely, as a public relations exercise, again surely, would not such an expense for the railway be a mere drop in the ocean in the general scheme of things? Why, indeed, DID it have to be so expensive?

Many exclaimed – with more than an element of justification – that the event was clearly a jaunt for the more affluent, or even for 'those with more money than sense'. Certainly, it was a fact that many high-ranking BR managers and BRB members were known to have been aboard and '1T57' did also come to earn a place in the history books not as 'The Final Steam Train', but more so under the unfortunate sobriquet, 'The Fifteen Guinea Special'. In that particular context, as an aside, the fact that there were about 50 seats that did go unsold on the day might have intimated something.

From what we read today, BR all along seemed to have decidedly mixed feelings about its initiative, but then it had spent the previous few years systematically purging the network of steam power and, of course, there were a number of individuals on the Board who were known to be vehemently anti-steam. Notwithstanding all of that, it was also an undeniable fact that some considerable effort had been put into the 'behind-the-scenes' organisation and planning, in order to ensure

that the event really turned out to be a success in the end.

The major issue was that five operational steam locomotives had to be retained on the books until week-ending 17 August 1968. This of course, was merely a technicality, for neither before nor after the event, were any of these to be permitted to perform any other duties. But it was all the more fortunate that neither Lostock Hall nor Carnforth motive power depots had completely closed on 5 August and particularly insofar as the coaling and watering facilities were still in-situ and operational, along with enough personnel to perform the tasks to be required of them.

Behind the scenes, special posters headed 'British Rail Runs Out Of Steam', had already been distributed and now special commemorative tickets and brochures were being printed, with restaurant car staff being rostered to work overtime on a Sunday to serve the at-seat service of lunch, high-?tea and other refreshments.

Resulting from the various light-engine movements of the previous Sunday evening, of those five engines still in service, 'Black Five's Nos 45110 and 45305 were sat at Lostock Hall and sister engines Nos 44781 and 44871 along with Britannia No 70013 Oliver Cromwell were at Carnforth.

On Saturday 10 August, No 70013 was lit up again and during the evening, following completion of all the necessary checks, the Pacific started to make its way light-engine to Lostock Hall, where it would again be coaled, watered and made ready to depart once more the following morning. The two 'Black Fives', Nos 44781 and 44871, were also lit-up during the day, in order to play their own later roles in the activities.

Fortuitously, perhaps with the hindsight gained the previous Sunday, two engines had been prepared by the steam-raisers at Lostock Hall. Although the fully lined-out and immaculate No 45305 had all along been the preferred machine of choice, it was soon observed that the fire-grate had fallen in, causing stand-by No 45110 (equally well-presented and in lined-out livery), to be rostered. In the gathering gloom, these two were soon joined by Oliver Cromwell and, surrounded by lines of other now long cold and lifeless hulks, stood awaiting their final hours of glory and the coming opportunity to earn

their places in the history books.

And so it was that, at 05:38 the following morning, No 45110 set out light-engine with a Preston crew, heading via Wigan for Edge Hill Depot, where it arrived at 07:20. At 08:36, another Preston crew moved No 70013 off shed heading in the direction of Manchester, arriving at 10:00. Over at Carnforth, at around the same time and coupled together, Nos 44781 and 44871 were slowly backing off-shed to set out towards Hellifield, where they would reverse direction in order to run northwards to Carlisle. The Special Traffic Notices of the period indicate that although the West Coast Main Line over Shap had been closed the previous weekend, it was open on this date. It is, therefore the more curious that the light-engine movements this day did not run over Shap.

The driver of No 44781 was Charlie Wilson, his fireman was Jeff Beattie and they were accompanied by loco inspector Bert Moore (all three being Carnforth-based men). On

No 44871, was driver Willie Pape (an ex-Carlisle man) and fireman John Gorst (both of Carnforth) with acting footplate inspector Frank Watson

RIGHT Travelling at 50mph, high on the valley side past Mallerstang Common, Carnforth's 'Black Fives' Nos 44871 and 44781 climb with 1T57 on the final stage to Ais Gill Summit. With the roadway far below, this is one of the remoter stretches of track, but close to where the unfortunate tragedy of September 1913 caused the deaths of 14 passengers, when a southbound express passed a signal at danger and collided with the rear of a stationary train (from Accrington MPD).

Meanwhile, at 'centre-stage' back in Liverpool, electric No E3083 was soon dropping the 10 coaches of very mixed-livery empty stock down the 1-in-93 into Lime Street station and passengers beginning to present their commemorative tickets at the barrier in order to board. In light of a shortfall in bookings, one vehicle was deleted from the originally proposed 11-coach set. No 45110 had already been waiting at Edge Hill for half an hour and, amid huge crowds lining the platform ends watched over by a solitary BTC policeman, now slowly backed onto the other end.

Having coupled-up and now crewed by Edge Hill driver Jack Hart and fireman Brian Bradley, departure was but a single minute after time at 09:11, and, with some initial rear-end assistance from E3083, No 45110 slowly set out up the incline with its 364½ tons to head for Carlisle. There being a number of high-ranking BR managers and BRB members on board, apart from the fact that the event would, undoubtedly also be closely followed by the media, the loco inspector accompanying the train was no less than John

Hughes, Chief Inspector for the British Railways London Midland Region and this gentleman was to supervise operations from one or other footplates throughout the day.

1T57 was to cover 314 miles during its 10¾ hour journey and special stops for the benefit of photographers were made during the first stage at Rainhill, where the original 'locomotive trials' were held by the Liverpool and Manchester Railway in 1829, and at

nearby Parkside, where the Rt Hon William Huskisson MP, was killed in an accident following the opening ceremony of the Liverpool and Manchester Railway on 15 September 1830.

In order to witness such a uniquely historic event, crowds lined the trackside at both locations. Prominent in the background of most photographs taken at Parkside, was the shining Huskisson memorial. An absolute contrast was evident in early 2008, the monument all but forgotten and with heavily overgrown undergrowth and trees almost obscuring it from view.

Upon arrival at Manchester Victoria, some six minutes behind time, No 45110 left the train and, there now being no operational steam facilities remaining in the Manchester Division, it had to run light back to Lostock

Hall shed for servicing. No 70013 was waiting and backed onto the other end of the train to take it forward for the remainder of its journey, a generous 25 minute station allowance permitting an on-time departure. The route now lay via Bolton, Blackburn, Hellifield and Settle, and thence over the 'Long Drag' to Carlisle. The driver working the stage to Blackburn was a Preston man, Harold Bolton, with fireman Tommy Gorman and the guard was John Weal. As 1T57 passed the sidings at Agecroft Power Station, one of the CEGB RSH 0-4-0 saddle-tanks was in steam and whistling its own farewell.

Assurances having been provided during the previous week by Blackburn station staff, that platform-end watering facilities were still in full working order, proved to be ill-founded and, upon arrival, the Britannia now had to be removed from the train in order to access a much faster-running supply nearby. This unexpected additional movement caused a massive delay, however, and Settle Junction was passed some 36 minutes adrift. The Blackburn crew now in control, driver Bob Grogan and fireman Raymond Watton, now found themselves needing to make up some time, and a decision was made to omit the water-stop scheduled to occur in the loop at Blea Moor.

The trip had clearly been well-publicised and, at the lineside, it seemed if the entire population of the North of England (and elsewhere) had turned out to bid their farewells. Blackpool on a Bank Holiday weekend was nothing on this! Cars were parked erratically absolutely everywhere, station platforms and line over-bridges packed with humanity, even the sheep presumably no longer felt safe! We joined in the mêlée. Surveying the number of cars jam-packed right under the arches (and in the shot), the view of Ribblehead Viaduct from the slopes of

Shortly afterwards, and within yards of the summit, the train reaches the head of the beautiful Eden Valley and crosses over the 75ft high Ais Gill Viaduct, one of the most photographed locations on the whole Settle & Carlisle line.

Whernside might have suggested that a new Battymoss branch of Tescos had just opened and that everything was free for the day!

We moved on, hoping for a little more solitude higher up and further from civilisation. Hopeless! Cars and people were everywhere - the Sunday motorist brigade was out in force and driving at its usual pedestrian pace regardless of the urgency of others! Cresting the hill on the narrow, winding 'Coal Road' above Dent station, we came upon that never-to-be-forgotten vista of absolute gridlock. Bedlam! Very clearly, we were going to make no further progress whatsoever for a while in that direction, so, hastily abandoning our vehicle, we made directly across

the boggy moorland in the direction of the former water-troughs. Our mad dash being somewhat hastened by the chime-whistle soon heard in the far distance, a somewhat unsatisfactory 'grab-shot' was the best that could be obtained. (Nevertheless, no-one else was in the picture!)

For passengers, there was a planned lineside photographic stop alongside the isolated signalbox at Ais Gill Summit. Word of this had got out, however, and the location being, at 1169ft above sea level, the highest point on any main line in England, it proved to be a magnet for spectators. Those that had arrived early, now causing massive traffic jams on the narrow B6259, literally swarmed across the tracks and prevented any further chance of photography. It really was a case of the best shot being one of the crowds, not despite them – oh, and there might have been a train in there somewhere!

Still running late, a decision was

made to cut seven minutes from this brief sojourn and, as soon as the tracks had been safely cleared, No 70013 proceeded upon its way. Long after its departure, however, the highway alongside remained totally blocked with stationary traffic and the AA and RAC were going to be busy for hours rescuing numerous vehicles that had become bogged-down in the soft verges, or had totally expired through overheating in the queues. One thing was for sure, it ·was by no means certain that the way north would finally become clear until at least the return working had passed and, as about 60 of us had a prior appointment to partake in afternoon tea at the Temperance Hotel in Kirkby Stephen, most turned round to make the enormous (but faster) detour via Garsdale and Sedbergh. In retrospect, looking at the photos I did get, maybe that was where I should have headed in the first place! After all, I did already possess far happier memories of the 'Long Drag' along with the photographs to support these.

Perhaps the most vivid memory that many of us might retain of that sultry afternoon may well have been the impromptu football match between the North Yorkshire Moors Railway and the Severn Valley Railway that occurred on a far from level stretch of moorland immediately above the southern portal of Birkett Tunnel!

Arrival at Carlisle was some 33min late at 15:29, but by cutting the station time down to about 15 minutes, some of the lateness came to be reduced and, now with Nos 44781 and 44871 at the head, 1T57 set out again to retrace its route back to Liverpool. The driver of No 44871 was Norman Ashton and the fireman Tony Helm with Chief Inspector John Hughes accompanying them. Aboard No 44781 were driver Ray Grimshaw and fireman David Greenhalgh, with footplate inspector Bert Moore.

These Preston crews had travelled up to Carlisle 'on the cushions' on the morning Manchester-Glasgow (1S45). With two engines in perfect mechanical condition, along with the sultry conditions that afternoon, very little exhaust was evident as the train bowled along at something approaching 50mph all the way to Ais Gill Summit.

Cromwell returned light-engine some 15min behind the train, heading to Lostock Hall for servicing. Still

LEFT In a scene dominated by the imposing masses of Simon Fell and Whernside, a scheduled water-stop at Blea Moor, one of the few remaining operational water-columns on the Settle & Carlisle, is extended to a photo stop, this ably superintended by a mere two BT police officers and a single lookout man. Blea Moor is home to one of the loneliest of Britain's signalboxes lying some 3/4 mile from the nearest road adjacent to open moorland, where it bears the burnt inclement winter weather.

crewed by driver Grogan and Fireman Watton with acting Footplate Inspector Frank Watson, these men worked the engine through to Blackburn. After 1T57 had passed on its way, those few who lingered for a while on the hillsides in the vicinity of Mallerstang Common - perhaps reflecting upon the fact that they really had just witnessed the end of an era - could not help but to notice just how insignificant the Britannia appeared, as it almost silently passed through the glorious valley in the hazy afternoon sunlight. Dramatic scenery certainly, but without a steam engine working hard against the gradient, not even the noisiest of diesels could ever come even close to exuding the atmosphere. Most of us thought this was our last time here, we wouldn't return. Many didn't.

No 70013 took on coal and water at Lostock Hall as planned, after which it departed at 21:30, running to Doncaster shed via Blackburn, Copy Pit, Todmorden and Wakefield, now with a Healey Mills crew and a Leeds locomotive inspector. Although this movement was supposed to be a secret, we all knew that the locomotive was en route to Bressingham Gardens for preservation.

Fo the Blackburn-Bolton-Manchester Victoria leg and, afterwards, to return the light engines back to Carnforth, on No 44871 driver Ted Fothergill (of 'Belfast Boat Express' fame) took over.

He was accompanied by fireman Malcolm Thistlethwaite, one of Carnforth's celebrated Thistlethwaite brothers. The other brother, Ian was also present, firing No 44781 for Carnforth driver Jack Simpson and accompanied by loco inspector Bert Moore.

For the final stage, onwards from Manchester Victoria, via Earlestown, to Liverpool (Lime Street), No 45110 had leisurely returned from coaling and watering at Lostock Hall and now with Lostock Hall's driver Ken Mason and fireman Dick 'Roger" Owen in charge, set off running only about five minutes behind booked time. In no time at all, the final 30 miles or so were rattled off and, as the 'Fifteen Guinea Special' arrived at its destination at 19:59 some 9 minutes behind schedule, the sun was setting literally on the train and figuratively on the very end of an era. People everywhere were not quite so merry.

After the ECS had been removed at Lime Street, No 45110 lingered at the buffer stops of No 5 platform for some time, as though reluctant to depart the scene, finally moving very slowly out before a strangely silent throng of observers. As it drew away, fireman Roger Owen shouted, "No more dirty hands!" The engine returned light directly to Lostock Hall, withdrawal from service and, as believed at the time would inevitably occur, the last journey in convoy to the scrapyard.

Ironically, although 1T57 may very well have been the last train to be worked by a British Railways-owned steam locomotive, it wasn't the last steam locomotive to leave Lime Street – indeed only a few weeks were to pass before.

No 4472 Flying Scotsman also came to depart, on 26 October and, more importantly perhaps, also heading for Carlisle! It was to be many more years before something like that would happen again – but happen again it would!

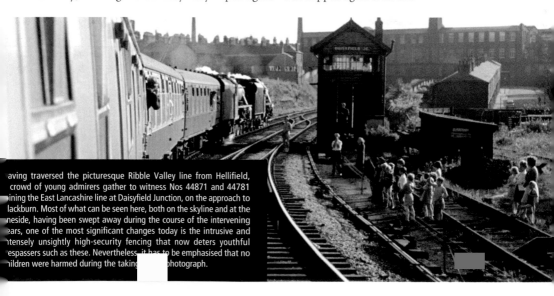

aving traversed the picturesque Ribble Valley line from Hellifield, crowd of young admirers gather to witness Nos 44871 and 44781 ining the East Lancashire line at Daisyfield Junction, on the approach to lackburn. Most of what can be seen here, both on the skyline and at the neside, having been swept away during the course of the intervening ears, one of the most significant changes today is the intrusive and tensely unsightly high-security fencing that now deters youthful espassers such as these. Nevertheless, it has to be emphasised that no hildren were harmed during the taking of this photograph.

Chapter 20

"Perchance it is not dead...but sleepeth"

After 4 August 1968, officially no further steam movements over BR metals occurred (apart from, that is, those in connection with the following weekend's 'Fifteen-Guinea Special'). Off the record, however, that was not quite the case. It has, nevertheless, taken 40 years to finally dispel some of the myths of 'ghost' steam happenings that emanated from all three of the final depots, the tales of some of which are still being told today and, of which, many grow ever taller as the years go by.

Doubtless, there were a number of clandestine happenings that, essentially, had to be just that, for fear of being halted should the upper echelons of management have got wind of them. That being the case, some, in fact, went totally unrecorded anywhere. Notwithstanding that, those detailed below definitely did happen.

One such seldom-reported steaming occurred on Thursday 8 August and some four days after the end of steam. At Rose Grove shed (which, at the time, was still open for diesels), Stanier 8F No 48773 was lit-up again by driver Winston Hartley and moved around the yard for watering and coaling, in preparation for a light-engine journey to Bescot and thence onwards to Bridgnorth, Severn Valley Railway. Unfortunately, however, management, in the shape of Preston Control, got wind of the plans and the engine never got beyond the shed limits. Control reminded Rose Grove that there was

Rose Grove, August 1968. With connecting rods neatly tied to their running-plates, rows of withdrawn 8Fs await their final journeys from which there will be no return.

now a ban in place preventing any further steam locomotives operating over BR tracks. No 48773 was, therefore, placed safely back inside the shed, with the instruction that its connecting rods were to be removed to prevent any further recurrence. Some time later, on 13 September, the 8F did move again, and did reach the SVR by rail, but this time it was towed by a diesel to Tyseley and then on to Bewdley.

Regardless of the official edict, some shed-masters and managers became quite adept at bending the rules … if only to make life easier for everyone. Well outside the jurisdiction of Preston Control, on 24 August, the now privately-owned 'Black Five', No 45428, journeyed light under its own steam from Leeds Holbeck shed to its new home at Tyseley. It had spent almost a year since withdrawal awaiting such a move and, still bearing its tangerine-painted 55A shed plate, it was seen that day taking water in Derby station.

On 20 September 1968, the prob-

The scene at Lostock Hall on 10 August 1968. There are at least 25 withdrawn locomotives in this view.

ably deliberately sparse information available today suggests that another hush-hush move occurred in moving Standard 5MT No 73050 in steam from Manchester to Peterborough. The Rev Richard Paten had purchased the, then sole preserved member of the class for £3,000, its scrap value. His intention being to display it on a plinth outside the local Technical College, ultimately the locomotive was found to be in such good condition that there was resistance to this idea and it eventually found a home on the Nene Valley Railway. On 15 November 1968,

Jubilee No (4)5596 Bahamas worked in steam from storage at Bury electric car sheds to its new home at the Dinting Preservation Centre.

There were other movements of main-line locos by rail that year, these including several 'Black Fives'. No 45025 went from Carnforth to the Hunslet Engine Co in Leeds and then to its first home on the Keighley & Worth Valley line, No 45110 went from Lostock Hall to Ashford and No 45212 from Lostock Hall to Keighley. During the week between the 4th and the 11th of August, No 44888 was also sent to

Derby for a BR open day there. It was still there three months later, but eventually quietly disappeared for scrap. All of these movements were 'out-of-steam' and behind diesels. However, much later, in travelling back from Ashford to Bridgnorth, on 17 August 1970 at Bescot Depot, the coupling-rods were replaced back onto No 45110 and the engine worked forward from Bescot in 'light steam'- in fact pushing the accompanying Class 40. Once on the Severn Valley line, it might be added that, with pressure rapidly falling on the final stretch downhill to Bridgnorth, the tender contained nothing but spare fire-bars and fresh air, all the coal having been used up!

The following year, another example of an in steam movement was that of the, now preserved, J27 0-6-0 No 65894 from the NCB works at Philadelphia to Thornaby MPD in 1969. The Divisional Maintenance Engineer, the late John Bellwood, not only drove it down the coast line through Hartlepool but, in order to turn the engine, he then took No 65894 over the Tyne bridges into Newcastle Central station in full daylight, to the amazement of waiting passengers! In October 1969, following its first restoration, NELPG members also steamed Q6 No 63395 at Thornaby depot and ran the loco up and down the yard, within shed limits, but on BR tracks, and even turning it on the depot's roofless roundhouse turntable several times for photographs. Indeed, the engine then moved to Grosmont on 25 June 1970 towed by a diesel but, once again, in steam. There were one or two more instances of movements by 'industrials' over BR metals, particularly NCB locos. The Lambton 0-6-2 tanks Nos 5 and 29 from Philadelphia for example, made various journeys towed in light steam, before eventually arriving on the North Yorkshire Moors Railway.

Of course, there were numerous other workings over closed lines, where a preservation society was still negotiating for purchase, for example from Bewdley to Hampton Loade on the Severn Valley line. IOW O2 0-4-4T No W24 Calbourne ran under its own steam on the island during a stock move, over then still BR tracks, in about 1970. One thing is for certain, the publishing of this article will, doubtless, reveal many other previously unreported happenings that, in some cases, blatantly occurred very much behind

"PERCHANCE IT IS NOT DEAD...BUT SLEEPETH"

the backs of authority!

Although the demise of BR steam had long been forecast, when the end actually came in August 1968, many of those involved with railways felt a distinct sense of unreality - it being extremely difficult to comprehend that steam really had ended – one week it was there, the next week it had gone. There was, of course, still industrial steam at work in a number of locations, and a few more engines soldiered on hauling engineering trains for London Transport, but, at most of these locations this, too, was in rapid decline. Remarkably, however, some survivors remained at work into the early 1980s – even on NCB lines. In addition, it should not be forgotten that, although BR had finished with standard-gauge steam working, for some years to come it would retain the 1ft 11½in gauge Vale of Rheidol tourist railway in West Wales, running from Aberystwyth to Devil's Bridge.

After 1T57 had departed from Carlisle on 11 August 1968, many of those who turned out to be involved in that sad occasion clearly felt that it really now was all over. Nevertheless, as came to transpire, it was only just

over a month later that, on 26 October, steam in the form of Flying Scotsman materialised in the border city. Alan Pegler, owner of the preserved Gresley Pacific since 1963, had adeptly negotiated an agreement with British Railways that assured that No 4472 would be kept employed on main line excursions well into the early 1970s and a special that had also originated in Liverpool, worked to Carlisle, this time over Shap Fell. Not only that, but on 1 June 1969, Scotsman headed yet a further special over Shap to Carlisle, this time starting out from its birthplace at Doncaster.

Outside the North West, there were other specials planned for No 4472, of course, but these occasional forays constitute the early beginnings of the main-line preservation era and do not really play a part in this account.

The last loco to leave Rose Grove in March 1969 was No 44899, a former 12A Carlisle Kingmoor loco transferred there in December 1967. It was collected in a convoy, including Lostock Hall's Nos 45444 and 45318, that had called en-route to Draper's scrapyard in Hull. The shed continued to be used as a stabling point for diesel locomotives for several months, until this facility

531.03 (alias No 44781) derailed in the Malayan Jungle near Bartlow, Essex. September 1969.

was transferred to a part of the remaining sidings area near the station. The depot building soon became derelict and was finally demolished in 1973, the site today being unrecognisable, as part of the M65 motorway now crosses it.

The situation over at Carnforth probably needs little further explanation. As at Rose Grove, diesels continued to use the premises here, until 31 March 1969, the remaining steam engines stored in the sidings gradually being towed away over the coming months. Several others had been purchased with a view to them being used on the hopefully soon-to-be preserved Plumpton Junction to Windermere (Lakeside) branch, being stored meanwhile at the depot. From Christmas 1968, two shed roads were leased for this purpose and as many as possible were then moved under cover. Following closure, the entire site

In the final three years of existence, no less than nine locomotives ending their days on 10D's allocation, found their way into preservation. 'Black Five' No 45110 saw purchase from an unlikely source, by members of the Flairavia Flying Club, based at the former RAF Biggin Hill airfield in Kent. The engine soon moved to Ashford for storage before ending up on the Severn Valley Railway.

The shedmaster's office, Lostock Hall, a typical feature of ex-L&Y depots - and former domain of Mr Mr Harold Sedgbeer. In 1988, this part of the structure, covering the offices, workshops and stores, still retained the typical L&Y 'sawtooth' roof, the remainder having been totally rebuilt in 1954.

The scene shortly after demolition. An overall view taken from Watkin Lane, surveying the scene by the site of 'Bowden's Gap'. Access problems preventing development, there is currently no other practical use for the site (although it will later be taken over as a gypsy encampment and even, at one stage, by a travelling circus), the mere outline of the concrete walkways between the filled-in inspection pits today still bears silent witness to the age of steam, albeit now through a rapidly-advancing forest of ever-encroaching vegetation.

was handed over - by now in sadly run-down condition - to a company that eventually became 'Steamtown Carnforth'. Although for many years an excellent collection of motive power was maintained here, at times faithfully exuding the air of an LMS loco shed, the Lakeside Railway eventually went its own way and some of the locomotives went with it. Others went elsewhere, but Steamtown, however, had been born, and was to come to be an important asset to the railway preservation movement, before it too finally closed in 1997. Following this, the site was taken over by the West Coast Railway Company, which still uses it as a maintenance depot, albeit with visitors no longer being accommodated other than on rare occasions.

At Lostock Hall, during this period, the rows of withdrawn and abandoned steam locomotives outside the shed, awaiting their final call for the cutter's torch, made visitors feel like they were intruding upon a mass grave. It was, in fact, to be another nine months or so after the closure to steam, before the final few went their way, with Nos 44894, 45017 and 45388 believed to have been the very last to leave – from any depot – on 28 April 1969.

However, as one of the photographs shown here so graphically depicts, for one withdrawn 'Black Five', a final job awaited. The plans for this, unfortunately, included a bizarre conclusion. The 'Fifteen-Guinea Special' celebrity, No 44781 ended its existence in the limelight in September 1969, as a major film-prop - ostensibly in the Malayan jungle during the state of emergency there in the early 1950s - but in actuality somewhat nearer to home, at Bartlow on the, then recently-closed, branch-line to Audley End in deepest Essex.

Having been sold to Columbia Pictures, No 44781 was disguised as a tank engine (most curiously, without a chimney!) for a scene in the black comedy, The Virgin Soldiers. The plans calling for the train, it was ostensibly hauling, to be deliberately derailed and 'wrecked' and, after the cameras had done their job, even though at least one expression of interest in preservation was made, recovery then proved to be prohibitively expensive and the loco was broken-up on site. Sadly, apart from its historical associations with the final steam passenger train of all, No 44781 would have been the only

"PERCHANCE IT IS NOT DEAD...BUT SLEEPETH"

long-wheelbase Walschaerts valve-gear 'Black Five' to have survived.

Back at Lostock Hall, even after these last few rusting relics of a past age had departed and the weeds started to grow between the abandoned sidings, the ghosts still lingered. Shortly before all the steam-age infrastructure was swept away, Bob Gregson was one of the few who cared enough to eventually came back to say his own farewell to 24C/10D.

Lostock Hall Revisited -
A closing tribute by Bob Gregson

Diesel locomotives continued to use Lostock Hall depot until 1973, when all motive power was transferred to the north of Preston Station, and it was then used as a Carriage & Wagon repair depot, following the closure of the old C&W Works at nearby Todd Lane South. The Preston breakdown train and maintenance vehicles were also still based here, until a fire destroyed a section of the roof covering six of the eight roads. The two remaining roads were partitioned-off from the roofless section and, there, the business of vehicle maintenance continued up until January 1988, when all opera-

tions ceased and the building was closed down altogether.

In April 1988, I decided to revisit old haunts. Having passed by countless times over the·years, I now felt obliged to pay my respects after so long an absence. It was a beautiful, fresh spring morning, similar to the one I experienced during my first visit of some 26 years previously, but with a silence more profound than that of 5 August 1968. For the first time in my life, I had the entire place to myself.

I passed through the opening by the old oil stores and entered this ruined temple of nostalgia. Memories of better times came flooding back, as I stood amongst the decaying wreckage. Nature was slowly taking over; young trees, plants and grasses growing in profusion, spreading a green shroud over the rusting steel and rotting timbers.

The partition doors to the old L&Y section were open and, here, apart from the atrocious work of vandals, I noticed very little had changed over the years. I walked across the yard to the shed-master's office, with its characteristic bay window façade and here, too, the vandals had been hard at work – papers, books and furniture being strewn across the floor and, everywhere, a sea of broken glass – indeed, not a window-pane intact! I passed through to the signing-on lobby and stood there awhile, in the gloomy silence, deep in thought; wondering how many generations of railwaymen had passed this way.

Visions of familiar faces from long ago flitted before my eyes. A sudden chill in the atmosphere awoke me from my grip of melancholy and I walked out into the warmth and sunlight – back into the world of the living.

I wandered along by the inspection pits, trying to visualise how it all had been in happier times. Everything of interest in the yard had long since disappeared; save for two decapitated cast iron lamp standards that once illuminated the water columns. These were originally gas lamps and had probably been there since the shed was built. And there they remained, still standing side-by-side, like sentinels, faithfully guarding the entrance to the very last steam shed, their withered arms pointing defiantly towards the encroaching mass of trees and vegetation.

The building was eventually demolished in January 1990. Today, merely the outline of the concrete walkways between the filled-in inspection pits bears silent witness to the age of steam. It is difficult to imagine that it once contained a busy eight-road engine shed, coaling plant and turntable etc, once having an allocation of 50 plus locomotives.

1968 marked the 50th anniversary of the end of the First World War, and I remember seeing footage of the old veterans revisiting the Flanders fields, and hearing comments such as, "It's changed a bit since then" and "Who will remember it when we've gone?" A similar theme was passing through my mind as I stood near the filled-in 'trenches' (inspection pits) at 10D.

For the railway enthusiast of the late 1960s, the passing of steam had left a great void, one that, we knew, the few preserved railways then in existence could never fill with quite the same authentic 'feel'.

The story of main line steam had been concluded ... or so we all then thought ...that is, until 15 September 1971, when a 'secret' trial run from Hereford to Newport proved to be the portent of much greater things to come. What arose as a consequence of that brave pioneering exercise is, however, as they say, quite another story!

The pictures in this book were provided courtesy of the following:

BILL ASHCROFT, JOSEPH BOOTH, TONY BOWLES, NORMAN CALLAGHAN, DAVE BRADBURY, JOHN BURNETT, MAURICE BURNS, BOB CLARKE, RICHARD DIXON, BOB DOWNHAM, CHARLES FINDLAY, PETER FITTON, JOHN FLETCHER, TONY GILLETT, ROBERT GREGSON, ANDY HALL, DAVID HARDMAN, TOM HEAVYSIDE, ERNIE HEYES, DEREK HUNTRISS, MICK KELLY, IAN KRAUSE, STEVE LEYLAND, DICK MANTON, EDDIE MAY, TERRY MILLAR, TOMMY MILLER, PETER NORRIS, MIKE POPE, KEN RICHARDSON, DAVE RODGERS, BRIAN SHARPE, MIKE TAYLOR, IAN THISTLETHWAITE, MALCOLM THISTLETHWAITE, DAVID TOMLINSON, PAUL TUSON, JIM WALKER, BILL WATSON AND FRANK WATSON.

Design & Artwork: ALEX YOUNG

Published by: DEMAND MEDIA LIMITED

Publisher: JASON FENWICK

Written by: ALAN CASTLE